A HISTORY OF
FURNITURE

A HISTORY OF
FURNITURE

Celebrating Baker Furniture
100 Years of Fine Reproductions

———•———

Text by Sam Burchell

Harry N. Abrams, Inc., Publishers, New York

Editor: Robert Morton
Designer: Ellen Nygaard Ford
Rights and Reproductions: Barbara Lyons

Note: The Publishers wish to acknowledge the kind and generous
assistance given by John C. Aves, who has supported publication
of this book with his knowledge and enthusiasm over the course of
several years. Additional thanks are due to Nancy Douglas, Kate
Kreitzer, Philip Van Suilichem, and Alex Mitchell.

The author was greatly aided by background research provided
by Public History Services (Gordon Olsen, Dr. Richard Harms,
William Cunningham).
The captions for this book were written by Robert Morton.

Library of Congress Cataloging-in-Publication Data

Burchell, S. C.
A history of furniture : celebrating Baker Furniture — 100 years of
fine reproductions / text by Sam Burchell.
p.   cm.
Includes bibliographical references and index.
ISBN 0-8109-3107-9
1. Baker Furniture Company—History. 2. Furniture—
Reproduction—History. 3. Furniture—Styles—History. I. Title.
NK2439.B38B87   1991
749.2—dc20   90-47603
                                                       CIP

Published in 1991 by Harry N. Abrams, Incorporated, New York

A Times Mirror Company

Printed and bound in Japan

Table of Contents

Introduction

In the United States, the second decade of the twentieth century was a time of far-reaching change in the area of furniture and the other decorative arts. New ideas, new enthusiasms, and new interpretations were coming to the surface, and they were to have an enormous impact on the entire American furniture industry, then centered in the Midwest and particularly in Grand Rapids, Michigan.

On a fundamental level, Americans were gaining a new understanding of the past and reassessing their taste. They began to look with more respect and appreciation at antiques and their place in American life. As early as 1920, this newfound enthusiasm for the craftsmanship of the past became evident. Shopping for antiques was becoming a popular pastime, and in the 1920s decorators' showrooms and even gift shops were beginning to feature them. Large department stores like John Wanamaker, Jordan Marsh, and Marshall Field were sending buyers to Europe regularly, and antiques—or imitations of them—were finding their way into American living rooms more often than they ever had before. Reproduction furniture was much in demand, and many small cabinet shops made high-quality products: Karcher and Rehm, for example, Vollmer, Pottier and Stymus, Kimbel and Alavoine. The wealthy were building impressive mansions in select suburbs of America, and they were filling their houses with these reproductions, usually in European styles.

The idea that antiques and artifacts from the past could have aesthetic as well as historical value had been developing ever since the Centennial Exposition of 1876 in Philadelphia, where a hundred years of American independence and talent were celebrated in an outpouring of patriotism. In the area of furniture and the decorative arts the exposition tended to emphasize European imports, for, traditionally, American antiques were often considered unimportant and noteworthy only for their historical significance. They were deemed too crude to be

A display of the New England kitchen at the Centennial Exposition of 1876, held in Philadelphia, showed an early interest in America's past.

of any artistic value and far inferior to European antiques, especially English ones. But at the Centennial Exposition, there were many welcome indications that a new approach to the American past was taking place. Ironically, the catalyst was American furniture manufacturing itself and its thralldom to the Industrial Revolution.

The unfortunate effects of industry on nineteenth-century American design were more than obvious in such factory pieces as John Henry Belter's imitations of French Rococo furniture in the 1840s. This ornate and mechanically made furniture, it must be said, was enormously popular with the general middle-class public and not without charm. However, it had extraordinarily little to do with the realities of contemporary America, and reaction started to build against the sort of excess it represented. Many people turned to the marvelous simplicity of the American furniture exhibited at the Centennial Exposition, especially the elegant Shaker pieces, which relied entirely on patient craftsmanship and perfection of design. As the years passed, admiration for American craftsmanship of the past grew more widespread, and enthusiasts became increasingly outspoken. Irving W. Lyon's *The Colonial Furniture of New England* was published in 1924; it was the first detailed examination of early American antiques and is still admired and regularly consulted. In 1925 President Coolidge himself appointed a commission to collect examples of the work of early American cabinetmakers in order to "create a still deeper and more abiding interest and respect for the work of our forefathers." The fine furniture maker, Baker & Company, a decade before its specialization in the reproduction of eighteenth-century English furniture, hurried to produce several small collections of American furniture: in 1922 a line of colonial furniture; in 1923 a Duncan Phyfe suite, copied from originals exhibited at The Metropolitan Museum of Art in New York; and in 1926 a popular line of Pilgrim dining room pieces. American antiques began to be taken seriously, and by the first decades of the twentieth century a good deal of tangible progress had been made in spreading a new point of view throughout the country.

To a large extent this appreciation of the past—along with some very real suspicions about the present—had been nurtured by a generation of young American designers and craftsmen convinced that the mandates of the Industrial Revolution were damaging contemporary aesthetics. The young rebels called for a return to antique craftsmanship and insisted upon a reaffirmation of the bond that had once existed between the artisan and his work. Men who operated machinery, they felt, had lost all personal contact with the product they made, and the human dimension no longer existed.

The young designers gathered under the banner of the Arts and Crafts Movement, which, however old-fashioned it may seem today, represented the avant-garde of the time. Based on European ideas, the movement was taken up aggressively by Americans, but in both Europe and the United States it was a reaction against the Industrial Revolution and the disappearance of the handcraftman. In England, painters like William Morris and art critics like John Ruskin encouraged a Gothic revival, which they interpreted as a romantic, pre-industrialized utopia where skilled artisans could create handmade work: furniture, fabrics, wallpapers, ceramics, everything. The movement envisioned the pleasant, if not entirely realistic, image of the happy craftsman, totally in harmony with his universe, handcrafting products far superior to the tasteless and monotonous artifacts relentlessly stamped out by machine.

*The dining room of Governor
Botetourt's house at Colonial
Williamsburg. The restoration at
Williamsburg, conceived as early as
1902 and begun in earnest in the
1920s, was the first large-scale effort
to preserve America's historical and
decorative arts heritage.*

Nostalgia for the past and the appreciation of early craftsmen inevitably led to a renewed interest in collecting and to the development of new areas for the collector. This was particularly true in New England, where American antiques were most abundant. The search for Americana was something unprecedented in American life, and the trend soon came to the attention of museum directors and curators. At The Metropolitan Museum of Art in New York City, for example, exhibitions of American antiques were being mounted with some regularity. An important antique silver show was held in 1911, and in 1922 there was an exhibition of Duncan Phyfe furniture. The splendid American Wing, in which interiors and furnishings from actual houses were arranged around a central gallery, opened in 1924 and created a sensation.

There were other important affirmations of the American past. In 1926 Henry Ford established The Edison Institute in Dearborn, Michigan. Here he built a museum and a country village that re-created the humble roots from which he had sprung. And in the same year a far grander treasure house of American antiques was being assembled by John D. Rockefeller, Jr., who began the restoration of the old colonial capital of Virginia at Williamsburg in 1926. The entire emphasis of this historical reconstruction was on the craftsman, his tools, and his techniques. About the same time, another American with enormous financial resources, Henry Francis du Pont, began a distinguished career collecting American antiques. This interest culminated in turning Winterthur, his family home in Delaware, into a museum of unsurpassed excellence and brilliance in the field of American furniture.

By the second decade of the twentieth century the preservation of the American past was well under way, and serious homage was being paid to the nation's early craftsmen. This was a turn of events immensely appealing to Hollis S. Baker, who in 1925 became president of the small furniture company founded by his father, Siebe Baker. As early as 1915, he and his new bride, Ruth MacClure of Newton, Massachusetts, explored the antique shops of Boston and the surrounding towns. With the nation's new interest in antiques, he sensed that Baker & Company and, indeed, American furniture manufacturers in general were poised at the beginning of a new and

A gateleg table from Williamsburg. The earliest furnishings for the restoration at Williamsburg tended to be English pieces of the period, because they could be acquired more readily. Gradually, American-made furniture and objects took their places. Colonial cabinetmakers had been busy almost from the first days of settlement, but identifying and finding their work took time.

A Dutch-influenced painted desk from the Hudson River Valley.

challenging era. The demand was growing for the development of sophisticated lines of reproduction furniture—English, French, and American. Future rewards could well be impressive, not only in terms of profit but in terms of artistic excellence. This was the dual aim Baker took pains to stress. In an article for *The Furniture Blue-Book* of Grand Rapids (November 1923) he highlighted the rising standards in the country as a whole and echoed the dictum of William Morris, "Have only what you know to be useful and believe to be beautiful." He went

on to say that "there is no better rule for the maker or buyer of furniture. . . . One of the joys of manufacturing is the creative aspect of the business. It is not so hard to make beautiful things where unlimited time and money can be spent. But to bring beauty within the reach of the average man is an even higher accomplishment. It is here that an opportunity lies in the furniture trade. As usual where a serious effort is made to fulfill a demand, those who accomplish this end are able to reap a financial profit—and on this ground it is possible to bring together our commercial instincts and higher ideals."

Baker was certain about the direction in which he wanted to lead the company. By duplicating the finest techniques of the past, he would bring appealing and artistic pieces of furniture to the attention of the contemporary consumer. He was committed, like the followers of the Arts and Crafts Movement, to the preservation of the fine craftsmanship of the past.

Because of that commitment, Hollis S. Baker found himself in England on a summer's day in 1935. For several years, he had been making trips abroad in what was to become a lifelong search not only for antique furniture but for general information about the history and manufacture of furniture itself.

Gordon Russell, an Englishman whose family owned a furniture factory in Broadway, Worcestershire, always remembered with pleasure that day when he first met Baker. The American, he recalled years later, walked into his office quite out of the blue, "told me he was a furniture manufacturer on a busman's holiday, and asked if he could see our works." Baker's frankness and enthusiasm appealed to him, and it was the beginning of a long friendship.

Russell (1892–1973) was to become one of the most prominent English furniture designers of the twentieth century. Schooled in the Arts and Crafts Movement, he added machine production to handcraftmanship in the belief that "the English tradition has always been to use the most suitable materials available in a straightforward, downright way." He later expanded his business to London, where he designed furniture in the International Style as well as sold Thonet chairs and furniture by Alvar Aalto. He became the first director of the British Council on Industrial Design and was knighted in 1955. These honors still lay ahead of him when he first met Hollis S. Baker.

"I liked him at once," said Russell. "He told me, among other things, that rather than completing his legal training he had entered a business started by his father, that their main demand at that time was for reproductions of English eighteenth-century furniture, that he was greatly interested in the history of the craft and had already collected a few pieces of antique furniture with a view to setting up a small furniture museum."

Baker explained that virtually his whole life had been devoted to furniture and that he had been involved with its actual manufacture and sale for many years. He had been president of the company for ten years, and at this point his interests were shifting away from business and manufacturing to scholarship and the study of the cabinetmaker's art. He wanted to learn about the history of furniture from the beginning and to study with care the old techniques for making it. This was by no means a hobby on his part; he was undertaking such research entirely for the future success of his company.

Among the most original native-American furniture designs were those of the Shaker sect, whose philosophy of life mandated a simple, unadorned, practical decorative style. These Shaker pieces are from the Elder's Room in the Brick Dwelling at Hancock Shaker Village, a restored settlement in Pittsfield, Massachusetts.

He was nothing if not eclectic, and he was interested in fine furniture from every era and from every culture. He explained to Russell that he was committed to bringing his customers reproductions of carefully selected pieces, created as much as possible as they had been in the past. Naturally, he had all sorts of questions: When did men start making furniture? What sort of furniture did they make? How long did it take to develop suitable ways of joining timber or even how long did it take to learn to saw trees into boards which could be joined? How was it that although mortise-and-tenon and dovetail joints were well developed in Egypt five thousand years ago chests were still being made out of scooped-out tree trunks in England until approximately 1500?

To understand the life of any civilized people, Baker knew, one must know something about the setting of their daily living. Social life, clothing fashion, and many other aspects of everyday life are revealed in the decorative arts of any period of history, particularly in the furniture. In short, the history of furniture is the story of people. As Italian cultural historian Mario Praz says: "Just as our primitive ancestor built a shapeless chair with hastily chopped branches, so the last man will save

Henry Francis du Pont, a passionate preservationist, formed the largest and richest collection of American decorative arts in the world at his estate called Winterthur, near Wilmington, Delaware. The Marlboro Room at Winterthur contains— among more than forty-five pieces of furniture—a rare Queen Anne sofa, a tea table, and a pair of roundabout chairs made in New York.

The Port Royal Parlor at Winterthur contains some two dozen chairs and tables made mostly in Philadelphia and all unmistakably modeled on designs of the great English cabinetmaker Thomas Chippendale.

from the rubble a stool or a tree stump on which to rest from his labors." He goes on to suggest that "even more than painting or sculpture, perhaps even more than architecture itself, furniture reveals the spirit of an age."

With ideas of this kind, the education of Hollis S. Baker began, and he devoted his life to the study of furniture from the days of the ancient Egyptians to modern times. He studied its history and its construction, the woods from which it was made, and the craftsmen who made it. Then, he duplicated the best of antique furniture for his customers. Beyond his business interest, however, he never lost his initial enthusiasm and curiosity about the "long pageant of furniture," a phrase he used in the introduction to his own book, *Furniture in the Ancient World,* published in 1966. It was a long and gorgeous pageant, and over the years he was one of its most devoted spectators.

The Long Pageant

Early Furniture

Because Baker's main interest was in learning about manufacturing and design, his initial focus was on the furniture of ancient Egypt. As he explained, "most of the traditional techniques of cabinet-making were perfected long before the beginning of the Christian era," and there was the added advantage that several hundred pieces of Egyptian furniture more than three thousand years old still existed, remarkably well preserved. Greek furniture, on the other hand, had not survived, and accurate knowledge of its design came only from painted representations on vases and plates.

One reason why Egyptian artifacts survived into this century was the Egyptian belief in an afterlife in which tables, beds, chairs, and other pieces of furniture were as necessary as they had been in life. In the tomb of the pharaoh Tutankhamun, discovered by Howard Carter and Lord Carnarvon in 1922, many magnificent treasures were almost perfectly preserved, and among them was a piece that has become one of the most famous chairs in the world: the throne of Tutankhamun. Although it is elaborately carved and decorated to suit its ceremonial purpose, it nonetheless exhibits all the features of the classic Egyptian chair: a carefully joined wood-frame structure, an open-seat frame with woven-rush surface, and remarkably graceful lines. The animal feet of the chair were raised slightly so they remained visible above the rush floor covering used in most Egyptian interiors.

Egyptian tombs such as Tutankhamun's have given us our earliest examples of the furniture maker's art, and clearly it is as art that it must be judged. In ancient times and various cultures, the terms "artist" and "craftsman" were synonymous. It has been, for example, and still is the aesthetic philosophy of the Japanese and their teachers, the Chinese, who make no distinction between the fine arts and the applied arts, and

This gilded chair belonged to the pharaoh Tutankhamun, who ruled Egypt some four thousand years ago. His tomb was opened in 1922, and many objects and some fifty pieces of furniture expressing the decorative style of the period were recovered.

it explains why so many ordinary objects used in everyday Oriental life are exquisitely beautiful. Pieces found in the excavations of ancient Egyptian tombs—chairs, stools, couches, tables, almost all the types of furniture we know today—demonstrate that craftsmen of the time understood a great deal more than simply the basics of furniture making. They were advanced in many areas like inlaying, veneering, and carving, and there is little doubt that most of these techniques fall into the realm of art.

In the classical world Greek art and furniture design were inspired by the Egyptians and, in turn, the Romans were inspired by the Greeks. As mentioned earlier, however, it is difficult to visualize Greek furniture, since almost none of it has survived. The knowledge we do have is limited to delineations on pottery and other surfaces. Much of what we know about Roman domestic life and interior design comes from the city of Pompeii, buried by the eruption of Mount Vesuvius in A.D. 79. Preserved for centuries under lava and not rediscovered until the excavations of 1748, Pompeii gave us Roman civilization almost intact, and its style of art and interior decoration had far-reaching effects on European design in the eighteenth century. Wealthy Romans developed sophisticated tastes for luxury, and these tastes led to the use of many different kinds of furniture developed by the Greeks and the Egyptians: tables, desks, couches, benches, bookcases, and other occasional pieces, many of them surprisingly modern in their simple, functional design. There was every reason to suppose that the splendid work created by the Egyptians and later the Greeks and the Romans would initiate a continuing tradition of furniture design in the West.

After the fall of Rome in the fourth century, however, a thousand years of darkness fell over Europe. During the Dark Ages little of note occurred in any of the arts, especially in cabinetmaking. The first rays of light came to western Europe around 1100, when crusaders returning from the Middle East brought with them a number of Islamic ideas and an appreciation of Byzantine architecture. The pointed arch, in particular, was popular in France and marked the way to the emergence of the Gothic style, which dominated European design for some four hundred years. It was responsible for much magnificent architecture and

Because even early furniture was made of wood, examples have rarely survived. What we know of it often comes from images carved in stone or painted on vases or walls. This stone bas-relief sculpture from fourth-century Greece shows the god of healing, Asclepios, sitting on an imposing throne decorated with a snake motif.

furniture design, though at first almost everything was built for the church. The cathedral, not the home, was the center of social life.

Two groups nevertheless furthered the development of domestic furniture. A growing middle class, composed of rich merchants and comfortable burghers, wanted substantial and permanent furnishings for their homes, while the nobility, traveling back and forth between castles and places of pleasure, had considerably different needs. Furnishings for the nobility had to be portable; cupboards and chests were either disassembled or made in sections, and they served as trunks or crates

This elegant chair, probably made of ebony, and decorated with gilded panels and ivory, is only twenty-eight inches high. Its size suggests that it was made for Tutankhamun when he was a child, perhaps near the time he ascended the throne at the age of nine. It was buried with him when he died about ten years later.

for transporting goods. This kind of furniture remained portable well into the seventeenth century. The nobility led a nomadic existence, and furniture was carried in the baggage trains of kings and courtiers on their flamboyant periodic travels. Like other household goods, pieces of furniture ranked as "movables," a definition still honored in the French and Italian words for furniture: *meubles* and *mobili*. Furniture itself contributed little to the interior design of a room; rather, much depended on the tapestries, velvets, silks, and carpets that draped the walls, beds, tables, and chairs.

By the fifteenth century the Gothic style had become almost universal in Europe and strongly secular, and the best examples of it were found in central France, northern Spain, and southern Germany. Great centers of trade formed, and Flanders was one of the important areas for the manufacture of arts and crafts. During this period one of the most universal pieces of furniture was the household chest, which served many different purposes. Basically it was a trunk used to store

Relief carving on this stele from Meky Mont in Egypt shows the form of high-back chair common in the region during the eighteenth dynasty.

Paintings on a funerary chest designed to hold clothing for the deceased to use in the afterlife reveal a similar black-painted wooden chair of the time.

This Greek vase showing musicians reveals a form of stool made of wood with a laced seat.

clothes, tapestries, and other possessions and a traveling box for carrying these items on a journey. It was also used as a seat, a bed, or a table.

In the waning years of the Gothic era, the first elements of the Renaissance style began to emerge. The Renaissance marked a dramatic rebirth of culture and the arts, and the beauty of Greek and Roman architecture, interior design, and cabinetmaking was rediscovered at last. This glorious resurgence took place for the most part in Italy, spreading rapidly from its origins in Florence to Mantua, from Urbino to Milan, from Venice to all parts of Italy. There was new activity in architecture and in the arts of painting and sculpture as well as in furniture design and the other decorative arts. Lavish palaces reflected the sophisticated tastes of the Renaissance princes, who were as interested in the acquisition of art as they were in the acquisition of power. One of the most typical pieces of Renaissance furniture was the *cassone,* or clothes chest, generally elaborately carved and painted and often part of a dowry. In general, furniture developed to suit the needs of an aristocracy with new demands and new interests. It was no longer a movable item, and extravagant furniture became a permanent fixture in the great palaces and castles of the Italian city-states for the storage

The form of chair called a klismos *is here pictured on an amphora dating from about 430 B.C.*

The Gemma Augustea, *an exquisite onyx cameo of the first century* B.C., *shows the Roman emperor Tiberius triumphantly reclining on a bed or couch with a distinctive leg. Nearly two thousand years later, when Federico Maldarelli painted* The Pompeian Girl, *he almost certainly modeled the legs of her chaise longue and table on the* Gemma Augustea *or a similar source.*

Illuminated manuscripts from the Middle Ages also give clues to the forms of furniture in times when little other documentation was generated.

A small ivory carving depicts what beds looked like in medieval times and suggests that portability was an important factor.

of valuable objects, for comfort, as a status symbol, and to satisfy a taste for elaborate carving and surface decoration.

During the fifteenth century, Florence, where the Renaissance began, was the dominating influence in all the arts in Italy, cabinetmaking among them. The Medici family was largely responsible for the city's enviable position, and by the end of the century its members had sponsored the building of numerous churches, palaces, and country villas and patronized many artists. Second only to Florence in importance as an art center was the powerful city-state of Venice; its elaborate homes, churches, and splendid paintings can still be seen today in all their glory.

An engraving by Albrecht Dürer of the scholar Saint Jerome (opposite) probably tells us more about furnishings used in the fifteenth century, Dürer's time, than it does about what Saint Jerome really sat on.

This sixteenth-century Florentine carved walnut cabinet was clearly created for a person not only of good taste but also of substantial means.

William Randolph Hearst once owned this sculptured and gilded walnut cassone from late-sixteenth-century Italy.

Chinese furniture was little known in the West until the seventeenth century. This chair of the Qing period (about 1650) shows the soft lines and elegant lacquer finish of the best of its kind. The piece is in the Baker Study Collection at the Grand Rapids Art Museum.

The palaces in both cities were laden with sculpture, painting, tapestry, and the finest walnut furniture, examples of the most imaginative and painstaking craftsmanship. Luxurious inlay work in multicolored woods was one of Italy's great artistic achievements during the period.

After the gradual decline of Florence, the Renaissance reached its apogee in Venice and Rome. This period of the High Renaissance exhibited far different characteristics. In Florence, for example, during the Early Renaissance, furniture had been noted for a certain simplicity and purity of line, and emphasis was on the horizontal. Curves were often used, particularly in a popular artifact like the Savonarola chair, an X-frame decorated with classical motifs and based on an ancient Roman design. But this sort of simplicity was left behind as the High Renaissance developed in the early sixteenth century. Accumulation and excess ruled the day. There were overpowering accumulations of paintings, tapestries, and sculpture, of manuscripts and gold plate, all reflecting the grandeur and luxury of the times. Furniture followed suit, and the High Renaissance saw much elaborate inlay work, along with

gilded and painted tables, chests, and chairs. In a sophisticated city-state like Venice the heights of elaboration were reached in omnipresent lavish furniture with carved decorations and bas-reliefs of cherubs and scrolls. Similar elaborations were popular in Rome, though taste in that city was far more grandiose. Yet all the arabesques and scrolls came to an end in 1527 when Rome was sacked by the marauding armies of Emperor Charles V, and the city was looted for eight violent days and nights.

Baker's faithful interpretation of Italian Renaissance style renders the feeling of the credenza.

No matter how splendid High Renaissance furnishings and decorations may have been, however, it must never be forgotten that these were luxuries reserved almost entirely for kings, nobles, and the very wealthy. In fact, for centuries furniture had been the province of the rich and the privileged. This was true of the Egyptians, the Greeks, and the Romans; it was true of the northern European merchants of the Gothic period; it was true of the great Italian city-states of the High Renaissance. Even as late as the sixteenth and seventeenth centuries, any kind of sophisticated furniture in Europe was made either for the church or the nobility. Many splendid styles developed; the Baroque, which reached its perfection in Germany and Holland, produced chests and tables that were covered with elaborate moldings, caryatids, and obelisks. However, little of this sort of design and decoration was found in other classes of society, even in the middle class. The tastes of the seventeenth century, which saw the splendors of Versailles and the Louvre in France, were presided over by the aristocracy and the nobility. In fact, not until the eighteenth century did furniture begin to be "democratic" in any sense of the word or available to even the average middle-class consumer. This was the golden age of furniture making, particularly in England and in the United States, when the best of furniture reached a far wider public than it had at any other time in world history.

A seventeenth-century German engraving of doctors at work reveals some details of the period's home furnishings. When real artifacts are missing, such clues have helped illustrate a view of furniture history through most of the ages of human craft.

The heavier feeling of Renaissance and later European furniture seldom finds its way into reproductions designed for today's homes, but Baker created a dining room suite in a seventeenth-century English style that complements certain interiors. In this model room, the furniture works well with a contemporary abstract painting.

The Golden Age

England

The hundred or so years from 1714 to 1830 was the great period of English cabinetmaking and furniture design. Although this is generally called the Georgian period, after the four English kings who reigned during those years, it is more important to know that a piece was designed by Hepplewhite or Chippendale or Sheraton than the fact that it was made during the reign of George III, for instance. The richness of the period in the area of domestic furniture is extraordinary, and there are no easy explanations for this. Of course, one can point to excellent craftsmanship, wealthy patrons, and fine materials, but these, elements were not unique to the eighteenth century. Nor is it enough to say that taste in England was extraordinarily refined, presided over by a cultured upper class that had been well educated at Oxford and Cambridge and that, in consequence, was thoroughly familiar with the classics. A university education and knowledge of the classics—and even a Grand Tour abroad to view the remains of antiquity and of the Renaissance—explain a good deal, but they do not explain the handsome interiors designed by Robert Adam nor those fine desks and chairs and commodes handcrafted by Thomas Chippendale and other talented cabinetmakers.

There is perhaps a less romantic, and a less aristocratic, explanation for the high quality of furniture design and production in England during these years. It was, above all, a century of wealth and discovery for England, an important turning point marking a period between the time when furniture was produced almost entirely for the palaces of royalty and the enormously rich, and the beginning of a new era when it was produced primarily for the homes of the upper middle class. It was hardly a move in the direction of democracy, but there was, in effect, a significant broadening of the consumer base, a shift that was to change the nature of cabinetmaking in Europe and America forever.

The graceful lines of a chair's back, arms, and legs—and the gently padded foot—express the delicacy and beauty of the Queen Anne style. This English armchair of about 1720 is made of walnut.

This piece from an early Baker catalogue shows a Queen Anne chest-on-chest of considerable finesse.

Furniture might not yet be for Everyman, but the pendulum was swinging in that direction.

The degree of artistry involved in furniture design was as remarkable in France during the same period, perhaps even more so, but in that country the talents of the best cabinetmakers were reserved for the king and the small coterie of nobles who surrounded him. This was by no means the case in England, where new influences and new ideas were coming into play, and prosperity was spreading to many different levels of society. The century saw the discovery of mahogany and the extensive importation of china and lacquered furniture from the Orient—events that had enormous influence on furniture design. Great country houses were being built one after the other, and the newly rich middle class was becoming more powerful and more demanding. Wealth was based on the rapid growth of overseas colonies and strong

From Baker's Stately Homes Collection, this fine Queen Anne bureau-cabinet is modeled after an original in the possession of The Right Honorable Lady Mary Howick, descendant of a family that traces its origins to William the Conqueror. The interior of the piece shows elaborate fittings and exquisite inlays; characteristic of similar furniture of the time, a sliding panel above the desk top reveals secret recesses.

From Ugbrooke Castle and the estate of Lord Clifford of Chudleigh comes this handsome Queen Anne kneehole writing desk in walnut.

Baker's interpretation of the Ugbrooke desk follows not only the lines of the piece and its precise fittings but nearly every element of its graining and inlays.

international trade. As a consequence, there was a large new segment of the population that needed houses, furniture, and decorations of all kinds.

With the ascension of George I to the throne in 1714, the great age of furniture design in England began in earnest. While in France the influence of the royal court remained as powerful as it had been in the previous century at Versailles, Britain had its own rising class of minor nobility and wealthy merchants who determined trends in the decorative arts.

Since neither George I nor his successors were patrons of the arts in the same sense as the French kings, artists and craftsmen could express their own individuality and creativity without being hampered by the dictates of the monarch and the court. Such freedom of expression brought many cabinetmakers into the limelight: Hepplewhite, the Adam brothers, Sheraton, and Chippendale.

George Hepplewhite did much of his work between 1770 and 1786, using simpler forms and less ornate carving than Chippendale. He was influenced by the furniture popular in the courts of Louis XV and Louis XVI, and many of his designs are often referred to as "French Hepplewhite." The brothers Robert and James Adam were architects who not only designed houses but, like many architects today, designed the interiors and the furnishings as well. Robert Adam traveled extensively in Italy, where the discovery of the ruins of Pompeii prompted a renewed interest in classic designs, and he brought this Neoclassical taste back to England. In addition to Hepplewhite and the Adam brothers, the other great British furniture designer of the period (though he was not a cabinetmaker and made none of his own furniture) was the Yorkshire preacher Thomas Sheraton. Characteristic of his furniture was the shield back chair, and his use of the acanthus-leaf motif carved on table pedestals was famous.

A mahogany side chair in the Chippendale manner shows characteristic ball-and-claw feet but a rather more unusual motif for the back—a central support that mimics silk ribbons with a rosette, a braided cord, and a tassel, a virtuosic feat of carving for any cabinetmaker.

Thomas Chippendale's dramatic contribution to English furniture style is expressed in this elaborate commode, made between 1750 and 1757.

In one of its early Manor House
showrooms, which presented pieces in
ensemble fashion, Baker displayed a
restrained but elegant Chippendale
dining suite.

Wollaton Hall, a Tudor palace built on a site occupied since the twelfth century, was long a home for the Middleton family, who acquired this low chest during the reign of George I.

Swan-necked handles, bold cabriole legs with carving on the knees, and an apron with foliage mark Baker's precise delineation of the Wollaton chest.

Edward VI, son of Henry VIII, presented Penshurst Place, which was already centuries old, to the family of Viscount De L'Isle, one of twenty Knights of the Garter and former Governor General of Australia. This magnificent display cabinet from Penshurst reveals the influence on Chippendale of Chinese decorative embellishments.

Distinctive Chinese elements in the Baker reproduction of the Penshurst piece are revealed in the pagoda-shaped pediment, the paneled doors with foliage and moldings, and the finely carved, shaped bracket feet.

However, of all the eighteenth-century English designers and cabinetmakers, the one whose name is most familiar today is Thomas Chippendale. Born in Yorkshire in 1718, he was the son of a joiner, and as a young man he was apprenticed to a firm of cabinetmakers in London. Within a decade he had his own shop, and it soon turned into one of the largest furniture-making businesses in the country. His work was renowned for exquisitely carved decoration, cabriole legs, and elaborate chair backs, and he was particularly famous for the exotic Oriental designs and lacquer work that came to be called "Chinese Chippendale."

In 1754 he published *The Gentleman and the Cabinet-maker's Director*. It was as popular with the wealthy as it was with the interested cabinetmakers, joiners, and upholsterers who subscribed to it. The first

edition had sixteen plates, along with many drawings of Chippendale's own designs for chairs and settees and for more imposing furniture like commodes, dressing tables, bookcases, library tables, and breakfronts. Future editions contained additional designs, and they quickly found their way to the Continent and even to the faraway American colonies. Chippendale's book concentrated on Rococo furniture, largely adapted from the Louis XV style. His designs were by no means original, but the book served to bring his name before a wide public and make him famous. Even today his designs are easily recognized and universally popular. People who know little about furniture or cabinetmaking are nonetheless familiar with Chippendale's name and reputation.

The sort of work at which Chippendale excelled can be seen in some of the records he kept. In a list of the furniture he had been commissioned to make for David Garrick's London house in Adelphi Terrace, designed by Robert Adam, the main bedroom had "Chinese" furniture, lacquered green and yellow, and red damask curtains; the drawing room boasted gilt mirrors on walls hung with printed paper and curtains of green damask. In the dining room were twelve chairs

This flamboyant Chippendale armchair, with French upholstery, sports unusual dragon-mouth front feet and pagoda-roof upper corners on its back.

covered in studded red leather and also a mahogany table that cost ten pounds, not an inconsiderable sum at the time.

The use of mahogany by the Georgian cabinetmakers cannot be overemphasized. A red-brown hardwood, it was originally called "Spanish" wood and came from the West Indies—from Santo Domingo and Jamaica, in particular. The wood was dense and heavy and lent itself well to carving. Later, another type of mahogany was found in Honduras and Cuba, lighter in weight and color, and, even later, what is

Port Eliot in Cornwall has been home for a succession of earls since the fifteenth century. In this reception room, distinctive Chinese Chippendale armchairs (the faux-bamboo and lacquered frames are giveaways) are combined with later pieces.

Two views of Baker's version of the Port Eliot chairs illustrate the painted bamboo effect and added floral decoration.

A Baker display combines a Sheraton
secretary with a Regency armchair
with faux-bamboo wood treatment.

Partly in reaction to the exuberant and exotic elements introduced by Chippendale, later English cabinetmakers responded with a more restrained feeling and the use of classical motifs. These three pairs of dining chairs are contributions by George Hepplewhite and Thomas Sheraton.

known today as "American" mahogany was discovered in Central and South America. At first Chippendale worked in walnut, but he soon turned to the newly discovered wood from the West Indies. By the middle of the century, mahogany had largely replaced walnut as the wood of choice for the finest cabinetmakers in England and on the Continent.

It is misleading, however, to think of Chippendale as the greatest of all eighteenth-century English cabinetmakers and furniture designers. His reputation was chiefly founded on one popular book, and the designs in it were largely derivative. He personally was no more than an average craftsman. He was, however, a fine publicist and a man of great business acumen, the head of a large and successful firm that furnished and decorated many splendid houses throughout the British Isles. His name may legitimately serve as a symbol of the English businessman-craftsman of the eighteenth century who catered to an acquisitive society composed of merchants, financiers, and upper-middle-class gentry.

Few private citizens today will dine in halls as large or magnificent as those at Knebworth House in Hertfordshire, but its Regency pedestal dining table has been copied by Baker.

Baker's version of the Knebworth table features a generous expanse of precisely matched sections of mahogany veneer with a finely detailed surrounding inlay.

Longleat House, seat of the Marquess of Bath in Wiltshire, is one of England's best-known and best loved stately homes. Much of it, especially the parklands and gardens, may be visited by the public. In a quiet corner of the library stands a handsome Regency writing table, dating from about 1815.

Two views of Baker's Longleat writing table reveal its sensitive proportions, unusual fiddleback end supports, and an amusing frieze of lion mask and ring brass handles, not all of which, of course, are functional.

France

Across the channel in France, the names of kings and palaces rather than those of craftsmen identified furniture during the Golden Age, and the art of cabinetmaking reached heights of complexity and elaboration rarely encountered in England. The fact that the names of the great French cabinetmakers—Meissonier, Riesener, Jacob, Oeben—were virtually unknown, at least to the English-speaking public, indicates something about the closed society of the French court. France, nevertheless, was the world capital of art, culture, and design. Every country in Europe, particularly England, Germany, and Sweden, looked to Paris and Versailles for ideas and inspiration, as did countries as far away as Russia, China, and the United States. In France fine furniture was clearly the province of the nobility. An army of *ébénistes,* woodcarvers, and cabinetmakers was required to provide furniture for the French court and to make the somewhat less ornate furniture that was being exported to foreign aristocracy in countries all over the world.

Furniture in France had long been a fine art, for a previous golden period had occurred a hundred years earlier under Louis XIV (1660–1700) at Versailles. The style of the Sun King and his court was largely determined by two houses, the Hôtel de Lambert in Paris and Vaux le Vicomte near Melun. The architect of both was Louis Le Vau (1612–1670), and the interior designer Charles Lebrun (1619–1690). After 1665 Lebrun designed complete interiors for the Louvre and Versailles, with all architectural features, furniture, carpets, and tapestries. The furniture was extraordinarily elaborate, the mark of French skill and the envy of the world ever since that time.

The French took furniture making seriously. Its production was ruled by guilds surviving from the Middle Ages, and every craft was rigidly controlled and defined. Originally, furniture and woodwork were the province of the *charpentiers* until the demand for goods of a finer quality led to specialization. By the middle of the fifteenth century, furniture and other portable wooden artifacts had become the concern of the *menuisier,* a word derived from *menu,* meaning "small." Toward the end of the sixteenth century furniture decorated with marquetry and

Obitus Regis Henrici ii. huius nominis: Parisiis ad Turriculas die x. Iulii, 1559.

TOVRNELLES

A. Regina plorans.
B. Cardinalis Lotharingus.
C. Magister equitum siue Connestabilis.

D. Cursores excurrêtes vnâ cum Medicis ac Chirurgis pariter, ex Flandria à Rege Hispaniarum missis.
E. Milites conducti, id est, Custodes Regis.
F. Medici ac Chirurgi.

In about the middle of the sixteenth century the fatal illness of the French king Henry II inspired an engraving depicting his medical treatment. The engraving shows the king's bed, with its ornate, carved canopy posts, legs, and headboard. Other furniture in the room is less dramatic.

veneer gained popularity, and the art of veneering in ebony was introduced into France from the Netherlands. The craftsmen who specialized in ebony veneering were known as *menuisiers-en-ébéne,* and later as *ébénistes.* By the eighteenth century, a single chair might have to be worked in turn by a joiner, carver, gilder, polisher, and upholsterer, each of whom was a recognized specialist. Other guilds relating to

A carver's delight is this amazing French armoire now in the Louvre Museum in Paris.

Ormolu (gilded bronze) figures prominently in this commode of the Louis XV period.

Gilded bronze, some ten different woods (including tulipwood, rosewood, and holly), marquetry, veneer, and inlay went into the making of this writing table for Madame de Pompadour, mistress to Louis XV. The distinguished cabinetmaker Jean-François Oeben was its creator.

furniture making included cabinetmakers, bronze casters, glaziers, and so on. In 1743 the guild ruled that each maker must stamp his work with his name, and that it should be stamped also JME (*juré des menuisiers-ébénistes*) to show that it had been passed by the guild for standards of workmanship and design. There were rules and conventions of all kinds that were eventually abolished during the French Revolution.

Indeed, France itself was a society of byzantine rules and conventions. Social life was organized by women who set great store by the conventions of polite conversation, and the innumerable chairs produced by court cabinetmakers and their subtle variations reflect this point of view. At the simplest level there were two sorts of chair: the *siège meuble,* which was large and stood against the wall, and the smaller *siège courant,* which a servant would bring up. Armchairs (*fauteuils*) had

This exquisite commode, richly inlaid and with remarkable sculptural ormolu, was designed by the great ébéniste Jean-Henri Riesener.

their arms set back to accommodate hooped dresses, and by 1740 there were two types: the *fauteuil à la reine,* with a flat back, and the *fauteuil en cabriolet,* with a curved back. The *bergère,* a tub chair with upholstered arms and cushions, was also popular, as was the *marquise,* a small settee, and the *canapé* (sofa).

   Protocol involving seats at court was rigid. Only the king could sit in an armchair, or even a *chaise,* a chair without arms. Courtiers argued and flattered for the privilege of a stool in public. The chair was an acknowledged symbol of authority, in England as well as in France. Consider the canopied chair of state, seen in the throne room in royal palaces (the Coronation Chair in Westminster Abbey is a good example) or the Speaker's Chair in the House of Commons. Even today the head of a committee is regularly called the chairman.

Going to bed as the king of France three hundred years ago was no casual matter; lords- and ladies-in-waiting, courtiers, servants, and other household staff were on hand to do your bidding. As a result, plenty of space was needed, as well as furniture of a type and style suitable to a lord of the realm. The ornate royal bedroom designed by Charles Le Brun at Vaux le Vicomte, which Louis XIV visited, typified the style of the day.

More remarkable than the ormolu mounts in this desk of the Louis XV period, possibly made by Riesener, are the delicate marquetry inlays of the drawer fronts, both inside and outside.

The reign of Louis XV (1723–1774) was a long one, and its furniture style was to have a lasting influence in many different countries. Straight lines virtually disappeared, and almost everything was curved, the curves themselves embellished with all manner of gilded carving and painted ornamentation. Rococo reigned supreme, and it was a period of elaborate excess. Exotic *chinoiserie* themes were commonplace, as was the period's characteristic *rocaille* ornamentation: scrolls and whorls, shell and flower motifs, and asymmetrical compositions of all kinds. The most exotic kinds of wood were used by the cabinetmaker: amaranth, palisander, rosewood. At least fifty different kinds of rare wood were regularly used in court furniture, along with Oriental lacquers and elaborate porcelain plaques inset into writing tables and small cabinets. There were new and unusual types of sofa broken down into special categories: the *causeuse, marquise, canapé à confidante, veilleuse.*

This commode in Baker's McMillen Collection is more restrained than many pieces of the Louis XV period, but distinguished by the double bombé curves of its front and sides.

The Metropolitan Museum of Art in New York counts among its many treasures the entire contents— including the paneling—of this room from a Paris residence.

When Louis XVI (1774–1793) ascended the throne, an entirely new sort of design became popular, and the classical influence apparent in England flourished in France as well. The political atmosphere had changed, and a certain austerity was in the air. Rococo curves and cabriole legs turned into straight lines, and Marie-Antoinette, extravagant though she may have been, influenced taste with her concept of restrained luxury. The Neoclassical style lasted until the French Revolution and then evolved into the Directoire style, which

French cabinetmaker Martin Carlin (who died in 1785) fashioned this delicate marquetry table with a marble top.

An atmospheric landscape typical of Chinese brush painting covers the bottom drawers of this remarkable Louis XVI–style desk, made by Riesener.

placed an even greater emphasis on the straight line and the sober use of classical models and motifs.

Because of the number of commissions, the court of Louis XVI needed even more cabinetmakers and other specialized furniture craftsmen than had ever worked at Versailles in the preceding century. In addition, the furniture was as involved as ever, even though the style was a trifle simpler than in the era of Louis XV. The flower motifs that flourished under the previous king now gave way to geometric lines and classical symbols: the scroll, the palmette, the Greek key. Along with new kinds of sofas and chairs came new types of commodes: the *commode à vantaux* (with tiers of drawers concealed behind doors) and the *demilune* (a chest with a curved front) among them. There were also small desks like the *bonheur du jour.* Such pieces were usually made of mahogany and ebony but copied in less glamorous woods like maple and walnut and sent all over the world, as the cabinetmakers of Paris hurried to sell their furniture to royalty and aristocracy from Russia to Portugal, from Scandinavia to Italy.

Not all furniture of the late Louis XVI period was ornate; this restrained cabinet in Baker's McMillen Collection is based on a piece of the period that foreshadows the relatively more severe lines of the Empire era.

From 1804 to 1815, Napoleon Bonaparte was emperor of France, and during his reign a style flourished that was characterized by classical lines and the introduction of decorative elements from exotic places. The Baker desk opposite features boldly carved lion's-head legs in mock ebony with gilt ornamentation.

The *ébéniste* Jean-Henri Riesener (1734–1806) is generally considered the leading cabinetmaker of the Louis XVI style. Born in Germany, he came to Paris as a young man and worked for the cabinetmaker Jean-François Oeben. He took over the business (as well as the master's wife) upon Oeben's death in 1763 and completed a number of projects Oeben had started, most notably the famous *bureau du roi,* the first rolltop desk, commissioned by Louis XV in 1760. In 1774, on the accession of Louis XVI, he was appointed royal cabinetmaker. Under the influence of Neoclassicism, his furniture became simpler and, in some cases, almost austere. He replaced marquetry veneer with plain mahogany, and the characteristic gilt-bronze mounts and drawer pulls of French court furniture were less elaborate in his hands. Yet even in the rarefied atmosphere of the French court Riesener's work was exceptional, remarkable for its great cost and the most expensive materials and rarest woods that he used.

After the French Revolution there was little work for a sophisticated and specialized cabinetmaker like Riesener, and he retired in 1801. The golden century of French furniture ended with the executions of Louis XVI and Marie-Antoinette in 1793, and during the years that followed the more severe Neoclassic style of the Directoire evolved. Somehow there was no longer a demand for great artists like Riesener nor the money to pay for them.

Instead, the Directoire style was a much simplified version of Louis XVI. A weak French economy demanded the use of less costly materials. Ormolu, for example, virtually disappeared. The Directoire style, however, was the preamble to one of the last great flowerings of French excess: the Empire style, created by Napoleon Bonaparte in the early nineteenth century for the glory of France and his own imperial crown. Even though he summoned some of the country's finest cabinetmakers and allied craftsmen, the style has always been notably uncomfortable, pretentious, and ornate, and the great days of French cabinetmaking appeared to be over—until perhaps the Art Deco era and the work of Émile-Jacques Ruhlmann. The Napoleonic style, however, did find a graceful reincarnation in some of the elegantly simple furniture patterned after it and made by Americans during the 1820s and 1830s.

Objects owned by notable men and women are often the only artifacts that survive over the course of time. This toilet chair was designed by Georges Jacob in about 1787 for a latticework bedroom at the Petit Trianon built by Louis XVI for Marie-Antoinette.

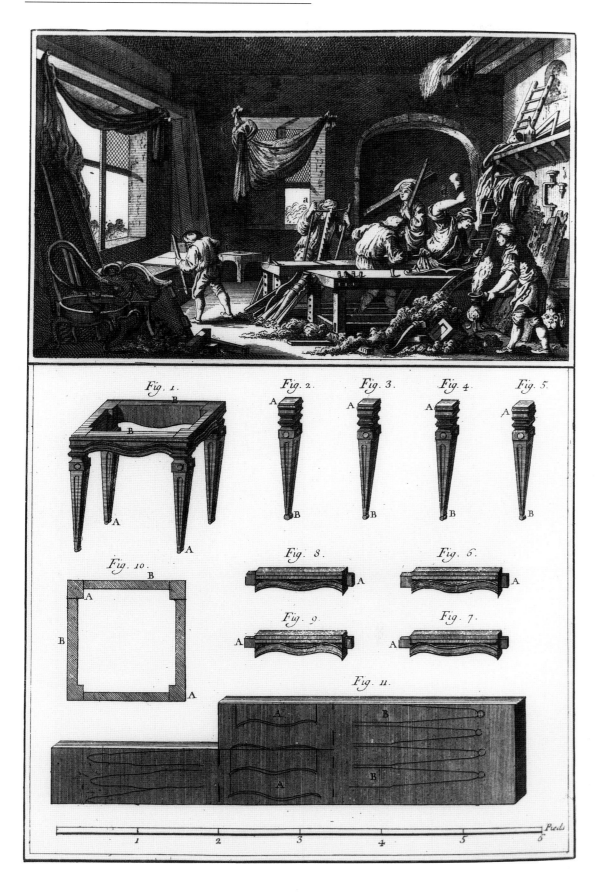

Among France's many great contributions to knowledge was the encyclopedia that Denis Diderot and his colleagues compiled in the seventeenth century. Details of what we know today about various crafts in France come from the engraved pages of the complete edition; this one illustrates some of the skills of the menusier, or cabinetmaker.

The two main woodworking skills in Colonial America were those of the joiner and turner, the former being essentially one who "joined" pieces of wood and the latter employing a lathe to "turn," or shape, wood. This chair from Plymouth, Massachusetts, made of New England oak and maple, seems sturdy and serviceable and yet has a certain flair added by its unknown maker. It was created between 1640 and 1660.

America

As a matter of fact, most styles popular in England and France did eventually reach America, first as an English colony and then as a young and independent nation after 1776. However, the new country's heritage was English, and English principles in architecture, furniture design, and the decorative arts continued to be dominant after independence. The styles, it must be admitted, often arrived in the New World long after they were fashionable either in England or in France. They were destined to change every twenty-five years or so, and they managed to take on distinctly American characteristics.

The Queen Anne style, for example, known as American Baroque, was not adopted in the colonies until around the 1720s. In some ways, designs were rather simpler than their English models, and this was to be characteristic of American cabinetmaking as a whole. Solid walnut and mahogany were used, and heavily veneered pieces were not generally made, no doubt owing to the fact that the colonies did not have craftsmen who were sufficiently skilled for the task. American chairs and tables in the Queen Anne style tended to have more delicate

*From Boston comes this unique
William and Mary japanned dressing
table, dating from between 1700 and
1730. Made of cherry, maple, and
white pine, the table is unusual in
having virtually every surface decorated.*

Most of the research on early American antiquities began in New England, and it was a long time before the craftsmanship of regional makers, especially those in the South, was recognized. The Museum of Early Southern Decorative Arts, in Winston-Salem, North Carolina, has been a pioneer in identifying, collecting, and cataloguing furniture of the region. This chest is in its collection.

An unidentified maker in Essex County, Massachussetts, fashioned this solid and handsome table with a folding top in the last quarter of the seventeenth century.

As time went by, a certain lightness of feeling entered early American furniture design; this piece from Pennsylvania, still clearly a product of the turner's art, shows a considerable amount of delicacy in its slat back and shapely armrests.

proportions than their British counterparts. Like English Queen Anne the American colonial version was based on the graceful curving line and elegant cabriole legs often ending in a ball-and-claw foot. Acanthus leaves and scallop shells were common motifs. Particularly in New York, Queen Anne had greater simplicity and lighter legs, though inlaid ornamentation was used extensively. The early years of the eighteenth century were prosperous ones for the thirteen colonies, and as in Great Britain a number of different kinds of furniture reflected their new leisure and wealth: dressing tables, card tables, tea tables, and those distinctly American combinations, the highboy and the lowboy. The highboy was a case piece composed of two parts: a stand fitted with drawers supporting a taller chest of drawers. The lowboy, on the other hand, was a dressing table similar to the highboy stand.

The Windsor chair, with its shapely, curving back and light spindle supports, has been a popular American standby.

By the middle of the century, colonial cabinetmakers were beginning to produce what is called American Chippendale furniture, and for the first time they were regarded as being uniquely American. All three editions of Chippendale's book *The Gentleman and The Cabinet-maker's Director* were studied with enthusiasm by American furniture makers. Relatively little furniture was imported because of the expense involved, and throughout the eighteenth century the publication of furniture design and pattern books allowed the colonies to mirror English taste, always within the limitations of a society that, even as a colony, did not have the self-indulgent upper classes and aristocracy found in the mother country. There was no call, for example, for the elegant and specialized marquetry and cabinetmaking that filled the palaces and great country houses of Britain. The Chippendale style, however, was in vogue in America from around 1755 to 1785, and came into its own around 1760, particularly in Philadelphia. The highboys and lowboys made here at that time are among the finest examples of American cabinetmaking, equaled only by the magnificent block-work furniture created by Edmund Townsend and John Goddard in Rhode Island.

Very early American furniture has seldom found its way into reproduction, but Baker boldly produced this gateleg dining table with simply turned legs. For homes of a particular decorative style it is an ideal solution.

Not surprisingly, when colonial households could afford something more elaborate than the local turner's skill could at first manage, the models for design came from England. And craftsmen in America soon became adept at fashioning their own variations on Queen Anne and later styles, many of them copied from imported English pieces. This Boston highboy of about 1725 is made of veneered walnut and maple with pine used as a secondary, or support, wood.

A passion for "japanning" (lacquering), and painting Oriental motifs on furniture, overtook American craftsmen as it had those in England and France. This Boston high chest of drawers was made between 1740 and 1760.

In the Winterthur Museum's Queen Anne Dining Room, shown above, Henry Francis du Pont artfully combined the bold curves of the furniture and the dramatic patterns of resist-dyed upholstery with panels of soft green woodwork from a mid-eighteenth-century house in Derry, New Hampshire.

Informal entertaining is suggested in this group of Baker pieces from Charleston, with a tea table set in a bedroom. The tester, or canopy bed, features rice stalk carvings on its posts, a characteristic feature of furniture from Charleston, where rice and indigo farming made the fortunes of the leading families.

This Queen Anne wing chair from New England, with needlepoint upholstery, dates probably from 1750.

The major colonial cities developed their own minor variations of the Chippendale style, and there is Boston Chippendale, Newport Chippendale, Philadelphia Chippendale, and so forth. Boston Chippendale, for example, was extremely plain, and its characteristic form was the *bombé*, or curved, chest. On the other hand, Philadelphia Chippendale was known for its elaborate carving and extravagant rococo lines. There was even a stripped-down version called Country

The stark simplicity of the lines of a 1740 Queen Anne side chair from Philadelphia contrasts with the intricate pattern of its back splat and the rather bold carving at the knees and on the top rail.

Baker's version of the tilt-top tea table, modeled on a Charleston, South Carolina, original conforms in every detail to examples in Thomas Chippendale's design book, copies of which were in Charleston barely six weeks after publication in London.

Chippendale that lasted as a style well into the nineteenth century in many rural areas.

Following the American Revolution of 1776 and the establishment of a new government in 1789, a neoclassical style of furniture called Federal appeared, and flourished from about 1795 to 1820. American cabinetmaking began to achieve a distinct flavor of its own. People began to consider the Chippendale style old-fashioned and were eager

A Chippendale tea table has a scalloped-edge top that tilts to permit the table to be stored out of the way against a wall. This Philadelphia piece was made about 1775.

Among the earliest and best of the identified cabinetmakers of Philadelphia is Thomas Affleck, who made this chest-on-chest in the days just prior to the American Revolution.

American cabinetmakers had an advantage over Europeans in being closer to the Caribbean sources of mahogany. This high chest, made by an unidentified cabinetmaker, probably from Philadelphia, is fashioned of mahogany, poplar, white cedar, and yellow pine, a wood seldom found outside the South and never in European pieces. Its ball-and-claw feet and elaborate pediment—with a unique, small shell drawer—mark it as being in the Chippendale style.

for the designs of George Hepplewhite and Thomas Sheraton. American craftsmen were also looking for something entirely different that would express the independence and uniqueness of their vigorous new country. The sculptural, rococo forms of the traditional Chippendale chair or commode seemed reactionary, while the neoclassical references to Greek and Roman design in the Federal style suggested those republican principles of the classical world that appealed so much to the founders of the new country; the new furniture was rectilinear in outline and restrained in ornamentation. American cabinetmakers produced light, delicate pieces, and their design vocabulary employed many classical images: lion masks, leaves, bowknots binding bunches of wheat, urns, festoons, and swags, along with the new national emblem, the eagle with spread wings. The clean lines of the Greek couch and the *klismos* were enormously popular. The *klismos,* familiar from its common depiction on Greek pottery, was an elegant chair with saber legs and a curving shoulder board. Throughout the centuries it has had enormous influence on chair design, particularly in the case of neoclassical styles like American Federal and American Empire.

Duncan Phyfe, New York's best-known early cabinetmaker, is believed to have made this Sheraton-style card table in about 1800. He created the window seat at left, one of a pair, in about 1825. Born in Scotland, Phyfe ran a business in New York for more than fifty years.

Of all the cabinetmakers who specialized in the American Empire style the most prominent—and certainly the finest craftsman of them all—was Duncan Phyfe (1768–1854) of New York. Born in Scotland, he came to the new nation at the age of sixteen and served as an apprentice to a cabinetmaker in Albany, New York. By 1792 he had made his way to New York City, and it was there that he established his business with a shop on Broad Street and later on Partition (Fulton) Street.

His name is forever associated with graceful American Empire furniture, a style based on both the English Regency style and the Empire style of Napoleon Bonaparte, modified for American tastes. His designs were frequently copied, particularly in Philadelphia and by other New York cabinetmakers. One of his most popular and enduring designs was a tripod-based pedestal table, derived from a Sheraton version of the British Regency style. Duncan Phyfe's variation was widely admired, and certain stylistic elements like carved fluting and foliate forms, along with ribbons tied in bows and carved American

The Federal style, characterized by
classical restraint, began about 1800
during the period of America's first
independent governments and persisted
until 1815. This sideboard of the
period was made in New York.

An interesting example of sophisticated design models being adapted by local craftsmen is this lady's dressing table of about 1800. Its basic configuration derives from Sheraton's Drawing Book, but an American eagle surmounts the central mirror and the two painted-glass panels beside it portray Commerce and Industry, leading virtues of the new republic and of prosperous Baltimore where the piece was made.

eagles, were common in his work. Although elegance and simplicity are the hallmarks of Phyfe, as time went on his American Empire style became heavier and more indebted to the French Empire style. His finest work can still be seen today in many of the rooms of the Old Merchant's House on East Fourth Street in New York City, almost perfectly restored to its condition when the Treadwell family bought it in 1835. Consider, for example, those popular carved window seats (really small sofas designed to fit into a window alcove), refined samples of an elegant form. The French influence on the American Empire style is pronounced, based on publications of French pattern and interior design books and the presence of numerous emigré cabinetmakers from France like Charles-Honoré Lannuier of New York and Anthony Quervelle of Philadelphia. There was also some imported furniture, the result of increased trade between France and the United States.

The form of this chair, whose makers are believed to be the Baltimore brothers Hugh and John Finlay, is modeled on a Roman version of the Greek klismos. The inspiration is clearly classical, a familiar motif of the new republic, which thought itself a rebirth of the Grecian ideal of a true democracy.

There were many centers for the making of fine furniture: New York, Philadelphia, Newport, Boston, and one of the best of them all, Charleston, South Carolina. During the eighteenth century there were about two hundred fifty active cabinetmakers at any given time in Charleston, and the records of one of them, Thomas Elfe, reveal that his workshop produced some fifteen hundred pieces of furniture during one eight-year period—a fantastic figure, considering the handwork involved. A gracious city where the aristocrats of the Old South gathered when "in town," Baltimore attracted furniture makers because of its fortunate location relatively close to the West Indies, and its ships could carry ample supplies of fine mahogany at low cost. There is no doubt that furniture was one of the first and one of the finest art forms practiced by the young American nation.

Even a brief consideration of furniture design and production in the eighteenth century shows that it was a period of unparalleled artistry and craftsmanship, not only in Great Britain and the rest of Europe but in the American colonies as well. It was truly a Golden Age of exquisite handwork and imaginative design, and the period lasted almost until the middle of the nineteenth century.

Like no other furniture of the period, Baltimore pieces of the early nineteenth century are characterized by the variety and verve of their painted surfaces. Thomas Renshaw, who made the settee above (painted by John Barnhart) and Hugh and John Finlay, who fashioned the pier table at right and probably are responsible for the chair on the previous page, were principal exponents of the style. Part of the popularity of painted furniture lay in its novelty and in the fact that a customer could commission scenes dear to the family's history.

Paradoxically enough, the groundwork of contemporary furniture design was laid in this Golden Age, and the neoclassical styles of the eighteenth century (Regency, Directoire, and Empire, for example) led to the clean and uncluttered lines of much twentieth-century furniture. It is also important to remember that by the middle of the nineteenth century the full effects of the Industrial Revolution were beginning to be felt, particularly in England. In terms of furniture, this meant that mass-produced pieces were going to a wider public, and popularity led almost inevitably to a dilution of "taste," at least as conceived in the aristocratic circles of the eighteenth century. The blessings of mass production along with its many problems were now to have profound effects on furniture design and production. Ways had to be found to blend the handcraftmanship of the eighteenth century with the techniques of mass production being developed in the centuries that followed. The creation of harmony between factory methods and handwork was to be one of the remarkable balancing acts of modern times.

Despite the considerable differences in their styles and finishes, a Charleston chair and a Chippendale tea table make happy companions, showing that good interior design need not consist of uniformity.

One of the imposing remains of Charleston's eighteenth-century past is Russell House. Above is the Music Room, where a Charleston chair is pulled up to a tea table. At left is Baker's interpretation of the chair, one of a large set, the originals of which are believed to have been made in Paris. Baker's version, like the original, has a chinoiserie scene painted on its back splat.

The Industrial Revolution

Though it had been long in the making, the Industrial Revolution finally came into its own during the early years of the nineteenth century. Only a few decades before, three-quarters of the population of Europe and America lived in a rural world of farms, dirt roads, and barge canals. Most wealth came from the soil, and everything, including furniture, was made as it always had been—by hand. Power was generated by wind and water, and transportation was mainly by horse or sail.

By the 1850s, however, it was a new world of iron, coal, and steam, of machinery and engines, of railroads, steamships, and telegraph wires. Advanced technology and rapid industrialization changed every field of endeavor. Great Britain, of course, was the acknowledged leader of the Industrial Revolution, but its effects were felt all over the world. Certainly the rush to mechanization in the United States affected the way almost every product was made, and furniture was no exception.

As early as the 1820s and 1830s, the nature of furniture making in the United States was changing dramatically, and mass production began in earnest. Lambert Hitchcock (1795–1852) of Cheshire, Connecticut, may well be considered the originator of the first factory furniture. The famous Hitchcock chair, based on a Sheraton design and decorated with colorful stencils, was mass-produced successfully, and it is still being made today. After an apprenticeship in cabinetmaking, Hitchcock went to work for a small furniture maker in Litchfield. By 1825 he decided to go into business for himself. He settled in a village some thirty miles from Hartford where he built a small brick factory at the junction of two rivers, near a forest with a plentiful supply of hardwood and pine. While he worked there, the village came to be called Hitchcocks-ville (now Riverton). He conceived the idea of making a chair out of interchangeable parts on a primitive assembly line. His factory's ground floor had lathes, boring tools, and other machinery (driven by a waterwheel in the river outside) to process the lumber and bend chair posts and back slats. On the second floor the pieces were bonded together with glue and then placed in a drying kiln. A probably apocryphal story relates that the finished chairs were thrown out of the second-story window into a waiting wagon for shipment to Hartford. They passed the quality control test if they did not break. What is undoubtedly true, however, is that before long Hitchcock's methods were producing fifteen thousand chairs a year that sold at retail price between 45 cents and $1.75 apiece. He was moving toward the future and foreshadowing the Grand Rapids and Chicago manufacturers.

While Hitchcock and other Connecticut innovators like Eli Terry, who made shelf clocks with wooden parts, practiced the techniques of mass production, the original thirteen colonies were expanding to the west. A large volume of household products of all kinds was desperately needed. Handwork was still the most common mode of production, but many new inventions were being used: steam-powered lathes and saws and veneer cutters, for example, which made production far more rapid than it had been only a few years previously. Technological innovation was the order of the day, and improvements came one upon the other. Yet there was a basic conflict: Would you rather have a lovely *klismos* chair handmade by Duncan Phyfe or one of those mass-produced pieces—standardized imitations of European originals—being churned out in the factories spreading across the land, particularly after mid-century? Of course, factory pieces were far cheaper. There were new machines for sawing, for planing and turning, for mortising and carving. There was hardly anything too difficult for these clever machines. What they could *not* do, of course, was imitate the quality of handcraftmanship.

The most compelling symbol of progress during the nineteenth century was the Great Exhibition of 1851, the first international fair of any significance, held in London's Hyde Park. Organized by Prince Albert, the fair was a hymn to progress, and its exhibits presented six million visitors with a dazzling panorama of wealth and accomplishment from all over the world. Perhaps the most incredible achievement of the fair was the building that housed it, the Crystal Palace itself: a true symbol of the age of technology, a prefabricated glass and iron building put up in four months, covering nineteen acres, and providing a million square feet of floor space. There were some three hundred thousand panes of glass set in more than five thousand iron columns and girders.

The Hitchcock slat-back side chair is a perennial favorite that has been in continuous production from the same maker for more than a hundred years.

Panes were delivered cut to size, and columns and girders were preshaped in Birmingham foundries and delivered by the new railroads, often in less than a day's time. Certainly this was mass production on the largest scale ever.

Those who visited the Crystal Palace, from Queen Victoria to the smallest boy with a shilling ticket, regarded the machine and its products with awe. But there were a few voices of dissent. Henri-Frédéric Amiel, the Swiss writer, had this to say about the exhibition and the future it foretold: "The useful will take the place of the beautiful, industry of art, political economy of religion, and arithmetic of poetry." Most who witnessed the incredible machines—the steam engine and the locomotive, the spinning jenny and the water frame, the power loom and the hydraulic press—were not so pessimistic.

While today we might be equally impressed with the machinery of the Great Exhibition, the aesthetic level of the wares would seem elaborate and derivative to us. In the Medieval Court, England proudly showed its Gothic revival furniture, and everyone admired the fussy Austrian exhibit with its ornate four-poster beds smothered in luxurious hangings. There was even a bizarre "high-tech" invention: an alarm bedstead that could propel the occupant out of bed and into a cold bath at a preset time. Not surprisingly, the most admired exhibition at the fair was from France, which offered glorious porcelains from Sèvres and Limoges, carpets from Aubusson, silks from Lyons, crystal, silver, and jewelry from Paris, and fine perfumes from Grasse. Unhappily, there were also endless imitations of Louis XV furniture in all its excess, with acres of carving and forests of cabriole legs.

In view of this general atmosphere of excess, it is perhaps not surprising that the Austrians did not show any of the Biedermeier furniture and decorative arts that had been produced in Austria and the German states in a brief period lasting from the Congress of Vienna in 1814 to the Revolution in 1848. Today the designs of the Biedermeier period are eagerly collected and duplicated, since their simplicity and elegance of line fit well with modern tastes. The style's name derived from a Gottlieb Biedermeier, a fictional character used in a Viennese journal of the day to satirize the middle class. The furniture itself was comfortable, unpretentious, and spare, particularly when compared to

On the left is an authentic Biedermeier side chair, made in Germany about 1825 of walnut veneer over pine, mahogany, and cherry. Beside it is Baker's twentieth-century version in cherry wood. Both chairs are in the Baker Study Collection at the Grand Rapids Art Museum.

the French Empire style then popular in the Austrian Empire and elsewhere in Europe. Biedermeier was Empire furniture stripped of its bronze mounts and exotic woods. It was generally made of plain cherry, birch, and walnut and, from bourgeois apartments to the palaces of the nobility, it was enormously popular.

The Americans, young and optimistic, had requested more space than they could possibly fill and so relied on innumerable pyramids of soap and mounds of dental powder in lieu of other products, though they did show Cyrus McCormick's revolutionary reaper. In the area of furniture they had very little to exhibit: some technically advanced pieces from the American Chair Company—rocking chairs, adjustable chairs, revolving chairs—and some handsome wicker furniture by John Tuph of New York. The French furniture made a great impression on the Americans, and when they returned from the exhibition they took up the Rococo Louis XV revival with enthusiasm, joining it to their rapidly growing technology and their beginning mastery of furniture production. It was not the happiest circumstance in the history of design.

This recently renovated 1870s
suburban New York home displays a
bench, side chairs, and table (in the
alcove) by Biedermeier matched with
a pair of Villa Gallia armchairs
designed by Vienna's Josef Hoffmann
in about 1913.

Nevertheless, this combination of technology and elaborate design did produce at least one talented furniture designer and manufacturer. John Henry Belter (1804–1863) has been rediscovered in recent years. For a long time his work and most of the work of other Victorian artists and craftsmen were overlooked. Yet Belter in his own way was one of the finest cabinetmakers in the history of design and an innovator of heroic proportions. Born in Germany, he came to New York City about 1840, and soon he had made a name for himself as a skilled craftsman and the inventor of several mechanical processes that allowed him to make the Rococo Louis XV furniture popular at the time rapidly, in quantity, and beautifully. He constructed plywood sheets in laminated layers and developed techniques to bend them into flowing

curves. Then, he used a mechanical saw that he invented to carve complicated florals and arabesques on these curved surfaces. Though a great deal of handwork was still required to produce Belter's final products, he managed to do away with much time-consuming joinery. The importance of Belter to his era is evident in the fact that almost all the Rococo revival pieces made in America were indiscriminately called "Belter Furniture." There was no greater tribute.

Accompanying the enthusiasm for Belter and his reincarnation of Louis XV furniture was also a movement in the direction of greater simplicity, a direction that led furniture design into the twentieth century. Many found the ideas of the English founders of the Arts and Crafts Movement more than congenial. They, too, were delighted to be

The Victorian parlor in England depicted in this genre painting shows much the same taste in overstuffed detail as its American cousin. Called The Last Day in the Old Home, *the picture, by Robert Braithwaite Martineau, dates from 1862.*

By the middle of the nineteenth century, the Victorian style, with its antecedents in the curves and naturalistic details of the Rococo, had permeated American household design. The result was ornate, heavily decorated furniture with flamboyant carving and dark woods. This rosewood bureau, by Mitchell and Rammelsburg of Cincinnati, dates from about 1865.

turning their backs on all the curlicues of the Rococo and the Louis XV style. They favored a sort of streamlined and simplified Gothic style, based on the mythical image of the Middle Ages conceived by A.W.N. Pugin, William Morris, and John Ruskin, where "happy" craftsmen lived free from the tyranny of the machine. The movement was carried to the United States in the pages of Charles Lock Eastlake's book *Hints on Household Taste in Furniture, Upholstery, and Other Details* (1868).

Rosewood, a favorite of the Victorians, finds an innovative form in this tête-à-tête, or love seat, of mid-century. The strong curves and thick carving of such pieces were often laminated or bent in steam molds, techniques of the Industrial Age applied to former handcrafts. This chair may be by John Henry Belter of New York, the most successful of the period's cabinetmakers.

Along with furniture designer Bruce Talbert, Eastlake developed the Modern Gothic style. It was a simplified version of the Neo-Gothic, a contrast to the involved revivalist styles of the early Victorian period. Eastlake's book also contained general advice about interior design, the construction and manufacture of furniture, and the selection of wallpaper, ceramics, draperies, jewelry—everything, in fact, that could be displayed and used in the home. It was reprinted four times in England and six times in America, where it had enormous influence.

One of the most marvelous houses of the Victorian period (now restored) is the extravagant house Mark Twain built for his family in Hartford, Connecticut in 1874. The outside of the wooden house is a gingerbread fantasy of turrets and balconies, of verandas and chimneys. Both the furniture and the interior design (by Louis Comfort Tiffany) are lavish and imaginative, and a good deal of fine Eastlake-inspired furniture can still be seen in the house, particularly in the mahogany bedroom where the author's daughter died. In spite of his agreement with the Arts and Crafts idea of homemade furniture, Eastlake did not

A Parisian domestic interior of 1877 shows an almost identical concern for surface decoration, exotic motifs, and overstuffed comfort.

The library of the Mark Twain house in Hartford, Connecticut, built in 1874, shows the characteristic decor of the Victorian age—a comfortable, if somewhat busy, interior. The home of the great writer is open to the public.

look down on efforts in the direction of mass production. "The division of labor and perfection of machinery have had their attendant advantages," he said. "It cannot be denied that many articles of ancient luxury are by such aid now placed within the reach of the million." These words clearly demonstrate the distance furniture had come over the course of the years.

Many of the exhibits at the Centennial Exposition of 1876 in Philadelphia were concrete reactions to all the ostentatious furniture that had been seen at the Great Exhibition of 1851 in London. One of the most popular exhibitors was the firm of Kimbel and Cabus from New York, which manufactured Eastlake-inspired furniture almost exclusively and supplied many pieces for Mark Twain's house. They

New York City's fashionable rich lived on or close to Fifth Avenue at the turn of the century (at least for the fall and winter months of the social season) and occupied rooms such as these. The most extravagant of them is the gallery (at right) of Mrs. William Astor's residence at 34th Street, seen here as it was in 1894.

favored the simple rectilinear line of the Gothic revival style that
seemed streamlined next to the rococo arabesques of the imitation Louis
XV furniture that had dominated the French booth at the Great
Exhibition of 1851. And it certainly was streamlined in contrast to the
work of John Henry Belter. Kimbel and Cabus showed an entire
drawing room of ebonized cherry at the Centennial Exposition with
dado, mantel, cornice, sideboard, pedestal, and sofa in the modern
Gothic style favored by Eastlake. One critic wrote that the display was
"rich and tasteful enough to rank it among the very best of the

Industrial methods more creatively employed were the stock-in-trade of the Thonet Brothers of Vienna, who created a dazzling array of bentwood furniture in a style that served first in European cafés and restaurants and then in private homes for many years. The sinuous forms of the pieces are reminiscent of the Art Nouveau style, but the clean lines and absence of surface decoration suggest a more modern feeling.

American exhibits in household art." Simplicity was in the air, for other comparably unadorned work received careful attention and an enthusiastic response at the Centennial Exposition: magnificently simple and elegantly designed Shaker furniture and some of the early and equally simple American colonial styles.

In Europe, too, simplicity in design was much admired. Michael Thonet (1796–1871) was a German cabinetmaker and designer, the developer of bentwood furniture, and one of the giants of modern industrial design. He can almost be said to have brought furniture making singlehandedly from the realm of handicraft into the industrial age. Like Belter, he experimented with laminating thin layers of wood to achieve elaborate furniture forms. Eventually, in Vienna, he patented a method for bending wooden saplings to mass-produce the distinctive low-cost "Viennese café" chairs that were eventually sold all over the world and have now been popular for over one hundred years. By 1855 he learned to make the chairs from the copper beech trees that grew so abundantly in Central Europe and were suited to bending. He steamed long rods of beechwood until they were flexible and then bent them into iron molds. Finally, they were sanded, stained, and packed for shipping. A simple side chair was made from six or eight pieces of bent beechwood screwed together, and the extraordinary result was a lightweight, durable, and amazingly strong chair without joints.

The ever-growing demand for the Thonet chair provides one of the great success stories of the Industrial Revolution. With his brothers, Thonet created the largest furniture factory in the world, and he had branches in most industrialized countries. No other company anywhere in the world approached the volume of export achieved by the Thonet brothers (*Gebrüder Thonet*) of Vienna. By the turn of the century their customers were being offered a thousand different designs, the biggest seller being the famous No. 14, one of the simplest and most elegant chairs ever made. It was first developed in 1859, and over one hundred million have been produced by firms with the Thonet name and perhaps three times that many imitations have been made, particularly in Eastern European countries. "Never before has something better been created," remarked the famous architect Le Corbusier. Thonet opened a showroom in New York City in 1873, and its exhibits at the Centennial Exposition a few years later furthered American interest in the product.

From the 1890s to the beginning of the First World War, the Arts and Crafts Movement took hold in the United States. The finest cabinetmaker of the period, now rediscovered and commanding the highest prices at auction—his personal 1903 sideboard sold at Christie's in 1988 for $363,000—was Gustave Stickley (1857–1942) of Syracuse, New York. Stickley visited William Morris in England in 1898 and applauded the theories of the Arts and Crafts Movement. His first furniture exhibit took place in Grand Rapids at the Furniture Exposition of 1900. His ideas were not particularly revolutionary, as revealed in his description of one of the chairs he made: "The piece is . . . first, last, and all the time a *chair,* and not an imitation of a throne, not an exhibit of snakes and dragons in a wild riot of misapplied wood-carving."

There was nothing complicated about what Stickley wanted to accomplish. As he said, he wanted to break away from factory-made imitations of European furniture and to use "only those forms and materials which make for simplicity, individuality, and dignity of effect." He showed his furniture at exhibitions all over the country, sent out catalogues, opened a New York showroom, and published a magazine. He called his version of Mission furniture "Craftsman," and the style

Seeking to achieve honesty and simplicity in furniture design, Gustav Stickley created pieces that were solid in structure, pure in form, and straightforward in their use of materials. Sometimes known as Mission furniture (largely because they announced their "mission" or purpose so plainly), Stickley called his work Craftsman furniture, and his company bearing that name thrived until cheaper imitators drove it into bankruptcy in 1916. Today, pieces by Stickley are highly prized.

was extremely popular around the turn of the century. He had imitators even in his own brothers, who started a firm in Grand Rapids where Mission-style furniture was made well into the early years of the twentieth century. When it came to be produced in quantity by Midwest manufacturers, Mission furniture was advertised as "clean," "simple," "honest." In 1903 the *Upholstery Dealer and Decorative Furnisher* noted: "The Mission style has taken this country by storm, and seems to have filled the place in America that is occupied by *l'art nouveau* in France and the Arts and Crafts in England." It was a sturdy republican style, much admired by the general public, and manufacturers in the Midwest were quick to seize upon it.

In the decade following the Civil War the furniture-making industry in the United States was growing rapidly. New factories were being built in many parts of the Midwest in towns like Cincinnati, Ohio; Muscatine, Iowa; and Grand Rapids, Michigan. As early as the 1830s furniture makers from the Eastern seaboard like David Wooster, Zephania Adams, and John Smith established shops in Grand Rapids, drawn to West Michigan by its timber, water power, and river and Great Lakes transportation. Others followed suit in the next decades. By the Great Exhibition of 1851 the firm of Powers and Ball in Grand Rapids had one dramatic order for ten thousand chairs and annual sales of more than $30,000, a significant sum at the time. The firm itself had only been in business some two years; W.T. Powers and E.M. Ball had established their small furniture factory along the shores of the Grand River in Grand Rapids in 1849. Now, in 1851, Ball could boast of being able to "throw whole trees into the hopper and grind out chairs ready for use." Perhaps this was a trifle exaggerated, but there was more than an element of truth in his remark.

Traditional cabinetmakers in New York, Boston, and Philadelphia could scarcely compete with the mechanization of their midwestern counterparts. After the Centennial Exposition in Philadelphia many of the Midwest furniture manufacturers began to copy Eastlake Gothic and copy it cheaply, and by the late 1870s the style was being regularly produced. The center of the furniture industry had moved from the East to the river towns of the Midwest. Chicago, even more than Grand Rapids, became a great center for furniture manufacturing as the nineteenth century progressed. Furniture, in fact, became Chicago's fourth-largest industry, and the city's central position and excellent railroads offered fine distribution.

By the end of the nineteenth century, the process of furniture mass production started by Lambert Hitchcock was far advanced. Factory methods had succeeded in bringing a new kind of specialization to the furniture business. Now cabinetmakers concentrated on chests and cabinets, tables, desks, and sofas, while turners made chairs and bedposts. Other experts were called upon: carvers and gilders, upholsterers and painters of "fancy" chairs. New inventions appeared all the time, like steam-powered woodworking machines that used a template to reproduce designs on wood. There were now four general categories in the rapidly growing furniture industry: expensive traditional cabinetmakers on the East Coast; moderately expensive and virtually custom-made furniture from such firms as Kimbel and Cabus; moderately priced but well-constructed furniture made in the Midwest factories in Grand Rapids, Chicago, and elsewhere; and cheap, poorly made pieces for the working-class customer.

By 1870 larger factories were employing designer-draftsmen. The days of the handcraftsman seemed to be coming to an end. Machine carving was commonplace with inventions such as the Eastern-made

The Tiffany Studios in New York were far better known for their stained glass than for anything else, but Louis Comfort Tiffany, like most great designers, was interested in an ensemble effect. He designed this chair, one of a set made of oak with stenciled velvet upholstery, in 1905 for the William Wrigley House in Chicago.

spindle carvers, introduced by the Grand Rapids firm of Berkey and Gay. By 1890, the value of furniture produced in West Michigan exceeded six and a half million dollars. Thirty-one Grand Rapids firms employed 4,347 workers, and machines for sawing, planing, turning, mortising, carving, and decorative incising allowed the mass production of European imitations and styles from the East Coast. Some were attractive and well made; others badly made and in the worst possible taste. All of them, however, were sold at moderate to low prices, and furniture was being made to suit every taste and every pocketbook.

The shift in American furniture production from individual craftsmen working with hand tools in small shops to the factory system and machine production was firmly established. Even at mid-century the Grand Rapids firm of Powers and Ball had organized many "little branches," where they sold their mass-produced furniture, a set of chairs for $2.50 and a bed for $2.00. Every year during the decade between 1870 and 1880 five new furniture firms opened manufacturing facilities in West Michigan.

Modern Times

As the twentieth century began, two conflicting impulses characterized furniture making, both in Europe and the United States: the thrust toward mass production and the desire for the authentic craftsmanship of the past. Sometimes, paradoxically enough, a "factory" look was achieved only through the most painstaking handwork. Witness, for example, the Barcelona chair of 1929, designed by Mies van der Rohe, where the sleek line and the use of contemporary materials strongly suggested high technology.

In modern times there has been furniture of every conceivable style and price. The development of new styles has usually been associated with specific designers: among them, Victor Horta and Émile Gallé in the Art Nouveau period, Charles Rennie Mackintosh of the Glasgow School, Émile-Jacques Ruhlmann of the Art Deco era, Mies van der Rohe of the Bauhaus, Josef Hoffmann of the Wiener Werkstätte, Frank Lloyd Wright of the Prairie School, the brothers Greene and Greene of California, Charles Eames, and Eero Saarinen, to name only a few.

Nevertheless, while new styles were being encouraged, carefully made copies of historic pieces were produced regularly to satisfy those who preferred antique styles. Baker Furniture excelled in this sort of reproduction, and by 1931 the first Old World Collection of Georgian mahogany pieces had appeared. For the next fifteen years the company concentrated on the reproduction of eighteenth-century European and American furniture. The company, however, did not ignore new design and reproduced the work of Joseph Urban during the 1920s, of Finn Juhl and Robsjohn-Gibbings during the 1940s and 1950s.

Furniture in the twentieth century falls into certain categories, largely based on the materials used: tubular steel furniture, sculptural forms in wood and molded plywood, free-form shapes in plastic. Perhaps the most common theme is the search for a functional and economical product utilizing the latest materials and techniques. Such an idea, of course, is far from being original. It had been the impetus behind the work of craftsmen as different as Thomas Chippendale and Gustave Stickley. Perhaps only those extravagant *ébénistes* who worked

Scottish architect Charles Rennie Mackintosh is considered a designer in the Art Nouveau style, but the geometric forms of this chair from 1900 suggest a much more modern turn of mind.

in the royal courts of Louis XV and Louis XVI ignored such human imperatives. The ethos of the machine age not only affected furniture materials, it also had an enormous influence on the spirit behind its design. Somewhat naively, one Belgian exponent of Art Nouveau, Henri van de Velde, put his faith in machines: "The powerful play of their iron arms will create beauty as soon as beauty guides them." As early as 1894 the revolutionary architect Otto Wagner insisted that a new style must emphasize "horizontal lines . . . great simplicity and an energetic exhibition of construction and materials" to be compatible with modern requirements of simplicity and directness. Designers in all areas of the decorative arts were becoming increasingly aware of the challenges of an industrialized society. One of the new society's most compelling

Antoní Gaudí, a Catalan architect and one of the Art Nouveau movement's most original creators, designed not only all the furniture in this Barcelona apartment of 1904–06 but the setting as well. The sinuous lines of natural forms found extravagant expression in Gaudí's work.

symbols was the Eiffel Tower, erected on the Champs de Mars in Paris between 1887 and 1888, a frank and exuberant statement of high technology.

Just after the turn of the century the American architect Frank Lloyd Wright (1867–1959) lectured on "The Art and Craft of the Machine," describing the age of the machine and praising its works extravagantly. As a young man, Wright was apprenticed to the innovative architect Louis Sullivan, in Chicago, who introduced him to the Arts and Crafts Movement. In designing furniture for the houses he built Wright pursued an elegant simplicity much admired today, and his early use of oak clearly shows the influence the Arts and Crafts Movement (in which that wood was used extensively) had upon him. Yet there was one important difference that distinguished him from the complete converts: Wright was enthusiastic about machine-made furniture and admired its sharp, straight lines. Critics have often remarked that the furniture he designed was angular and uncomfortable. Surprisingly, Wright agreed: "Somehow I always had black and blue spots my whole life long from all too close contact with my own furniture." Wherever possible, Wright used industrial methods to produce his furniture. This was hardly because he turned his back on craftsmanship. Rather, Wright saw factory methods as efficient ways to produce handwork in quantity.

At the same time that Wright was praising industrialization, many other twentieth-century architects and furniture designers continued to support the Arts and Crafts Movement's deprecation of it. In 1901 the first issue of Gustave Stickley's magazine, *The Craftsman,* came to the attention of two California architects, the brothers Charles Sumner Greene and Henry Mather Greene. At the time they were creating appealing California bungalow architecture and interior design. Although their work did show a number of Oriental characteristics, they were primarily influenced by Stickley and the Arts and Crafts Movement. While the furniture they designed for their far from simple bungalows was reserved for their wealthy clients and not available to the general public, their principles mirrored Stickley's own: elegant form, exquisite handwork and, above all, simplicity of design. Most of their furniture was made by Peter and John Hall in Pasadena, who

Vienna's Josef Hoffmann, who founded the influential Wiener Werkstätte in 1903, followed Mackintosh's linear style in making handcrafted objects of great distinction. Though he aimed to create furniture of quality that could be mass-produced, most of his clients were well-to-do.

were, along with Louis B. Easton and Harold Doolittle, among the few cabinetmakers in southern California at the time. However, a good deal of commercial furniture influenced by Greene and Greene was produced by manufacturers in the East and Midwest and found its way to California. It satisfied customers who admired the Mission style of the Greenes but could not afford their prices.

Of course, no period of furniture style follows the linear simplicity of a chart, and the taste that produced the Arts and Crafts Movement coexisted with Art Nouveau and many other styles. For some thirty years, from the 1890s to the beginning of the First World War, Art Nouveau was an imaginative and vigorous decorative style that swept through Europe and the United States, leaving its mark on everything from architecture to jewelry design. It went under many different names: *Jugendstil* in Germany, *Sezession* in Austria, *Liberty* in Italy, *Le Style moderne* in France, and *Art Nouveau* in England and America. Described by one critic as a "strange decorative disease," the style found its inspiration in the forms of nature and revealed itself in floral abstractions and swirling arabesques. There were many master

In 1925 the organizers of a huge exhibition of decorative objects in Paris had little idea that their show would spawn a new style, Art Deco, although the name was not coined until the 1960s. For the next dozen years after the exhibition, Art Deco furniture and decorative accessories were top sellers. Among them was this console by Louis Süe made of burl ash veneer and a structure of aluminum.

craftsmen and designers: Charles Rennie Mackintosh, Antoní Gaudí, Josef Hoffmann, Victor Horta, Henrí van de Velde, Émile Gallé, Louis Majorelle, and Hector-Germain Guimard, who created those charming entrances to the Paris Metro that still enchant travelers today.

After 1895, Paris was the acknowledged center of Art Nouveau. It seemed as if almost every flat surface in the city was being covered with floral motifs and the undulating shapes of peacocks. Much of the decor and furniture of the era survives, and some of the best *fin-de-siècle* interiors can be found in fashionable restaurants like Maxim's and Lucas-Carton. The cabinetmakers who worked in France during the Art Nouveau period were some of the finest in the history of design. Émile Gallé, who made both glass and furniture, was one of the period's most versatile artists and also one of the most successful.

Gallé (1846–1904), whose father ran a small ceramics factory near the town of Nancy, began his career as a glassmaker. In 1890 he founded the School of Nancy, a cooperative organized for the production of the decorative arts. The cooperative idea was significant since Art Nouveau was an attempt to make a complete design statement and create a unified look for everything from furniture to clothes and jewelry. The School of Nancy included glassmakers, bookbinders, and cabinetmakers, as well as many other different kinds of craftsmen and

Though the lines of many Art Deco objects are more strictly geometric than this chair made between 1926 and 1931 by Émile-Jacques Ruhlmann, there is no doubting its style. The designer called it Éléphant Noir.

artisans. Gallé himself became interested in furniture around 1885. Gathering together a large group of talented cabinetmakers—he himself was not a woodworker—he opened a small factory where he produced his own designs. The furniture that emerged was a riot of carved vines, leaves, and marquetry landscapes and, although produced in great quantity, it was virtually handmade. Before the turn of the century Gallé had shops in Paris and Frankfurt, as well as the showroom in Nancy. A London shop was opened in 1904, the year of his death, and the factory in France continued to produce furniture in the Art Nouveau manner until 1935. Another successful craftsman was Louis Majorelle, whose furniture in wood and forged iron and cast bronze has a vibrant and imaginative sweep. The style was elaborate and often led to excess, but its exuberance will always serve to conjure up those glorious and vanished years of the Belle Époque.

The Paris Exhibition of 1900 aroused American interest in the style. During the year photographs and drawings of the new French furniture appeared in numerous magazines, and manufacturers produced versions of Gallé and Majorelle pieces for the American market. The style was reasonably popular in the United States, but it was presented to the public in far simpler form than had been seen in Europe. It was brought to a large middle-class public by Midwest manufacturers like S. Karpen Bros. of Chicago and the Indianapolis Chair Manufacturing Company. American Art Nouveau furniture was frankly made for a mass market, and it lacked the artistry and individual craftsmanship that had made the creations of the Nancy factory almost one-of-a-kind works of art. Gallé used exotic and expensive woods, for example, which American manufacturers could not afford to do.

In any case, the style was never as widely accepted in the United States as it had been in France, and the public began to turn more and more toward simpler Mission furniture, with the manufacturers quickly following suit. This was a direction, of course, encouraged by designers and architects like Frank Lloyd Wright and the Greene brothers of California, not to mention Gustave Stickley himself. All of them rejected extravagant and ornate French furniture, which in their minds recalled a history of decadence and royal privilege, and they sought instead the simpler craftsmanship of the American past.

Before the Art Deco period, Ruhlmann was known for pieces that featured exquisite burled surfaces and elegant geometric inlays. The 1916 corner cabinet shown here, however, with a marquetry vase of flowers in ebony and ivory at its center, is unique in his work.

By the first decades of the twentieth century the American furniture industry was moving ever farther away from handwork, while craftsmen like Stickley and members of the Roycroft Community (founded in New York State by Elbert Hubbard in 1893) were encouraging it. In Europe, traditions of individual craftsmanship were strong, and complete industrialization was resisted with greater force than in the brash new country across the Atlantic, which embraced the machine age with adolescent ardor.

An example of this difference is the exquisite craftsmanship that emerged in Vienna during those last years before the final collapse of the Hapsburg Empire. It is one of the great paradoxes of history that some of the most modern trends in European art and design appeared against the reactionary backdrop of Imperial Vienna. Between 1900 and 1914 there was an explosion of avant-garde talent: painters like Oskar Kokoschka, Gustav Klimt, and Egon Schiele; writers like Franz Kafka and Karl Kraus; architects like Adolph Loos and Otto Wagner; musicians like Gustav Mahler and Arnold Schönberg, and many others.

One of Otto Wagner's best students was Josef Hoffmann (1870–1956), an architect and furniture designer. Though Hoffmann started his career as a follower of Art Nouveau he soon turned away from its floral convolutions to develop, along with other designers in Vienna, a style that was severe, geometrical, and abstract, quite antithetical to the French and Belgian versions of Art Nouveau. The furniture he created was largely for his own buildings, though it is interesting to note that he did design a few pieces for the firm of Thonet, which produced the famous Viennese café chair. In terms of the history of furniture perhaps Josef Hoffmann's most significant act was to help found the influential and prestigious Wiener Werkstätte.

Under the spell of the Arts and Crafts Movement in England, Hoffmann and others started the cooperative venture in 1903, and it flourished until 1932. In addition to producing furniture, the Wiener Werkstätte periodically exhibited the work of contemporary European designers like Charles Rennie Mackintosh of Scotland and Henrí van de Velde of Belgium, among many others. The significance of the group's activities and exhibitions was not so much that it followed any consistent design direction. Rather, the Wiener Werkstätte kept alive

artistic integrity and the merits of handcraftmanship. Until the First
World War the workshops produced furniture, leather goods, metal and
glass, and textiles, all designed in a geometric version of Art Nouveau.
After the war the products were more in the Art Deco manner, and the
style came to the United States in the 1920s, where it was received with
enthusiasm.

One of the participants in the Wiener Werkstätte was Joseph
Urban (1872–1933), who immigrated in 1911 to the United States,
where he began a career both as an interior and a theatrical designer.
He was chief designer of the Metropolitan Opera in New York for
almost twenty years, and he designed sets for the dramatic stage as well
as furniture for theaters, hotels, and private houses. His furniture
designs were rectilinear and geometric, often using silver or ivory inlays
in black stained wood. Like Hoffmann, he designed furniture for
Thonet, and some of his designs were produced in the United States by
Baker Furniture. One of his first projects for the company was a
bedroom group made of bubinga wood (a hardwood from West Africa,
similar to rosewood) with straight lines and silver-plated hardware—
quintessential Art Deco.

Many different styles led to the development of Art Deco. As a
leader of the Bauhaus, a precursor to Art Deco, Ludwig Mies van der

Rohe (1886–1969) played a major role. He was apprenticed to Berlin furniture maker Bruno Paul in 1905 and then went to the Munich architectural offices of Peter Behrens. There he fell under the influence of Walter Gropius, founder of the Bauhaus, a German design school, and the French architect Le Corbusier. Mies began designing furniture in 1926, his first piece being a cantilevered chair of tubular steel that formed a wide, smooth curve. His most famous piece was a leather and aluminum chair made for the German Pavilion at the Barcelona International Exhibition of 1929.

Later in his career he was director of the Bauhaus, located in Weimar from 1919 to 1928, in Dessau from 1928 to 1932, and in Berlin from 1932 to 1933, when the rise of Nazism forced many of its exponents to leave for the United States. It was in the vanguard of modern design; it used many factory products like chromium-plated tubes and polished plates. Like the Wiener Werkstätte and the School of Nancy, it placed an emphasis on the collective nature of design and production. In addition to Mies many important furniture designers came from the Bauhaus, including Josef Albers and Marcel Breuer. By the 1940s and 1950s, when many of these designers had made their way to the United States, their influence was great: simple lines and the elegance of the modern, functionalist aesthetic.

The Bauhaus and the Wiener Werkstätte were two strong influences that led to the development of Art Deco. Incidentally, it must be remembered that the term *Art Deco* was not used to describe the period until the 1960s; in its day the style was known as Art Moderne (or New Art) in the United States and, in France, as *Le Style 1925.* It flourished in the years between the two world wars and came to dominate all areas of the decorative arts: architecture and interior decor, the design of fabrics and porcelain, of jewelry and glassware, even of *haute couture.* Like so much else in the history of art, decor, and fashion, the style came to light in Paris. In 1925 the *Exposition des arts décoratifs et industriels moderne,* originally planned for 1914, opened at last. At the time, Art Nouveau dominated design, but this style with its streamlined and geometric forms clearly looked to the future. Yet, Art Deco showed the influence of the early years of the century, as much of its furniture evolved from the designs of the Wiener Werkstätte, its colors from the

Finnish architect Alvar Aalto designed this wood-and-plywood chair in 1930, continuing a tradition fostered by the Wiener Werkstätte in which designer, craftsman, and furniture production company worked closely together.

Ballet Russes of 1909, and its line and architecture from Cubism and the geometrics of the Bauhaus of 1919. It may have emerged during *les années folles,* the crazy years of the 1920s, but like Art Nouveau, it was another serious attempt (and the last in Europe) to develop a coherent and lasting decorative style that would apply in all areas of design.

At the Exposition of 1925 in Paris, two pavilions in particular defined the mood and techniques of the new style: one, designed by René Lalique and devoted largely to his glass and ceramic creations; the other, the *pavillon du collectionneur,* with rooms containing elegant furniture designed by Émile-Jacques Ruhlmann (1879–1933). Of the many remarkable artists and craftsmen working in France during the Art Deco years, Ruhlmann was one of the most talented. Today, the resurgence of interest in this period has made his furniture the most valuable and the most sought after of all. Of course, the same thing could be said about the 1920s and the 1930s, when his grace and purity of design were recognized immediately. In characteristic Art Deco style he made lavish use of marquetry and tortoiseshell; of rare woods like macassar ebony, amaranth, amboyna, and violet wood; of ivory, jade,

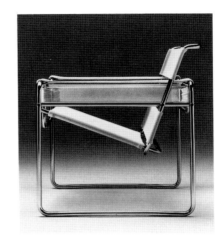

Another of the Bauhaus innovators was Marcel Breuer, who named this tubular steel chair "Wassily," for his great colleague and friend, the Russian painter Wassily Kandinsky.

Breuer also designed the tubular steel, leather-covered sofa shown here, and the standing cupboard.

and silver; of more contemporary materials like chrome and Bakelite. Certainly he was the most accomplished cabinetmaker in France since Riesener during the reign of Louis XVI.

Ruhlmann died before he had the opportunity of collaborating on the greatest artifact and finest joint endeavor of the entire Art Deco period: the French ocean liner *Normandie*. Work on the ship began in 1935, and no expense was spared to call on the services of almost every cabinetmaker, metalworker, silversmith, glass, and ceramic craftsman in France. Even in an era of great ocean liners, no one had seen anything so splendid, and in its brief career *Normandie* was a floating tribute to French style and taste, and to the Art Deco period in general. The magnificent ship was destroyed by fire in New York harbor at the beginning of World War II. Although some of the fittings and artwork survived, most are gone forever.

Art Deco had tremendous influence in the United States, particularly on furniture design. Designers of the time tried to suggest the simplicity and austerity of the machine age along with its movement, speed, and dynamism. Cubist geometry was an important influence on the style, and its symbols were compelling: the sun's rays, clouds racing in the wind, lightning bolts, greyhounds, automobiles, airplanes. Today the products of the period are eagerly collected, and the look of the 1920s and 1930s is extremely popular in Europe as well as in the United States. Many of the finest examples of the style have been preserved in cities like Los Angeles and New York, where splendid Art Deco architecture abounds. Numerous fine interiors have been preserved as well, particularly in New York. One of the most spectacular is Radio City Music Hall, where much of the furniture (along with fabrics, lamps, and wallpaper) was designed by decorator Donald Deskey. A selection of his designs was manufactured in the Art Moderne period by Baker Furniture.

The American public was first made aware of the avant-garde style—then called *New Art*—through exhibitions at some of the larger metropolitan department stores. Both Lord & Taylor and B. Altman in New York City held them, but the most significant took place in May 1927 at R.H. Macy in New York. Three hundred exhibitors were chosen from among the best designers and craftsmen in Europe and the United

Because of the region's long craftsman tradition of woodworking and the greater availability of wood in their native countries, Scandinavian designers became very inventive. Alvar Aalto designed this laminated and bent-frame armchair in 1947.

States. Sample rooms were decorated for the public to see, and among the interior designers were Josef Hoffmann of Vienna and Bruno Paul of Germany.

The popularity of the new style was soon noted by the furniture manufacturers of the Midwest. In 1925, Baker Furniture became one of the first American manufacturers to produce Art Moderne. At the January 1928 Grand Rapids Market Association show of some 450 exhibitors, Art Moderne influences were very evident, and the style was at the peak of its popularity in America. Further enthusiasm was added by the opening of the Museum of Modern Art in New York City in 1929, and by the fifteen yearly exhibitions of American Industrial Art held at The Metropolitan Museum of Art, starting in 1917. The Metropolitan believed that "our manufacturers and designers have not only the technical but also the artistic ability to produce objects of applied art of high type, especially on the basis of 'quantity production,' which is the only basis calculated to meet the requirements of current life." Particularly impressive was the eleventh exhibition held in 1929. It was planned by a group of distinguished contemporary architects, including Joseph Urban, Ely Jacques Kahn, Eliel Saarinen, Armistead Fitzhugh, and others. The Art Deco, or Art Moderne, style reached its maturity in 1939 at two impressive shows: the Golden Gate Exhibition in San Francisco and the World's Fair in New York City.

At the New York fair, however, it was apparent that other exciting developments were taking place in furniture design. The year marked the first time that a style known as Scandinavian Modern was brought to the attention of the American public. After World War II the style was to have a great impact on manufacturing and design in the United States. Designers from Denmark, Sweden, Norway, and Finland produced furniture showing the industrial age and mass production at its best. Scandinavian Modern developed from a strong tradition of handcraftmanship, and it was modern furniture that provided artistic excellence to a wide public at low cost. Furniture ranged from handmade wood to completely mass-produced pieces in metal and plastic. As it had with Art Moderne, Baker Furniture kept up with the times and presented furniture created by the Danish architect/designer Finn Juhl (b. 1912) who in 1945, in collaboration with the cabinetmaker

Danish designer Finn Juhl created this sleek armchair in 1945; Baker later commissioned him to create a number of pieces, which led to the introduction of Danish Modern style in the United States.

Niels Vodder of Copenhagen, created one of the finest examples of the lightweight modern chair in graceful and delicate wood. Juhl was one of the most prominent of the Scandinavian Modern designers and, like his colleagues, a strong believer in the idea of functionalism, a doctrine equating utility with simplicity with beauty. His innovative chairs consisted of a frame seemingly separate from seat and back which, while attached to crossbars, appears to float in space. He designed all manner of things: interiors, buildings, glassware, ceramics, carpets, and lighting fixtures.

One American designer who influenced Scandinavian furniture and in turn was influenced by it was Charles Eames (1907–1978), one of the foremost designers of the century. Like so many other furniture makers of the time, Eames was an architect as well as a designer. In 1937 he was appointed director of the department of experimental design at Eliel Saarinen's renowned Cranbrook Academy near Ann Arbor, Michigan. Colleagues and students included some famous names in American furniture design: Harry Bertoia, Florence Knoll, and Eero Saarinen, Eliel's son. At Cranbrook both Eames and the younger Saarinen began experiments with molded plywood that resulted in their famous designs of 1940 and awards for both men from the Museum of Modern Art in New York. In 1941 Eames moved to Venice, California, with his wife and collaborator, the designer and painter Ray Kaiser. After World War II (and following work with molded plywood for the United States Navy) he began to produce the first of a number of famous chairs—two molded wooden elements, seat and back, attached to a light metal frame that connects the two and also forms the legs. By 1946 the chair was in production, and he was honored with a one-man show at the Museum of Modern Art in New York City. Like Mies van der Rohe's Barcelona chair, it is one of the furniture classics of modern times.

One innovative furniture designer who produced a dining room and bedroom group for Baker Furniture in the late 1950s was the Englishman T.H. Robsjohn-Gibbings (1905–1976), today famous for satirical books like *Goodbye, Mr. Chippendale* and his many imaginative designs, among them a modern version of the Greek *klismos* chair.

Italian contemporary design, too, has produced its share of classics. Gio Ponti (1891–1971), architect, designer, teacher, and editor (he

Charles Eames, one of America's most innovative and progressive architect/designers, created these two chairs, one with a molded plywood seat and back, and the other formed entirely, except for supports, of molded plastic. Herman Miller, Inc., of Zeeland, Michigan, has manufactured both chairs since they were designed in the late 1940s and early 1950s.

Believing that a piece of furniture should express a sculptural totality, Eero Saarinen designed an array of molded plastic-and-plywood pedestal furniture in the 1950s. Manufactured since that time by Knoll Associates, which offers many other pieces by the great modern architect/designers, this chair reveals both a remarkable sculptural integrity and a pleasing aesthetic form.

founded the prestigious architecture and design magazine *Domus*) updated the austerely simple Italian *chiavari* chair from the early nineteenth century into a contemporary classic. Less traditional directions characterize Italian design today. Ettore Sottsass (b. 1917) makes highly unusual avant-garde furniture. He is perhaps best known for his industrial designs for office equipment that are functional and, surprisingly enough, quite in the mainstream of modern design. He created a sensation in the 1970s, however, with his cabinets and bookcases in bright colors and bold patterns, the equivalent of the hard-edged abstractions popular in art at the time. In 1980 he founded Memphis, a design group engaged in challenging conventional aesthetics with colorful, eccentric, and startling designs for furniture and other objects (lighting fixtures, metalware, and ceramics).

The same eccentric, avant-garde furniture is found today in Paris, as it is in New York and Los Angeles. In Paris, for example, furniture seems to be moving in several different directions at the same time. New directions are not always clearly defined. What is clear, however, is the direction in which design is *not* going. It is not going back to Versailles. One influential French interior designer, Andrée Putnam, applauds this rejection of France's royal heritage: "Classic French style, caught in the trap of its own history, stumbles over tassels, sneezes among velvets and brocades, dozes in fake Louis XV armchairs, and is suffocated by its overly rich past."

The French architect Le Corbusier once said that a house should be "a machine to live in," and this storage wall, lounge, and armchair could truly be described as mechanical devices.

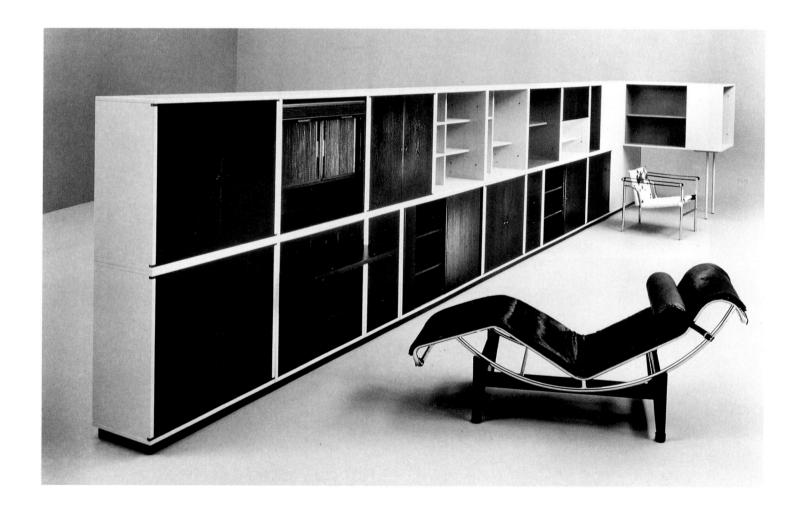

Even office furniture has come to be designed with flair and style. This Harter Martin Stoll D/6 pedestal armchair on casters has the adjustable features necessary in any seating equipment designed for an office worker.

In contemporary Paris the home is regarded as a kind of video entertainment, with flashbacks to the 1940s and 1950s and fast forwards to the age of halogen lamps and fluorescent colors. French design firms like Totem, Nemo, and the Italian Memphis are popular in the most up-to-the-minute circles. Memphis derives great pleasure from the fact that couturier Karl Lagerfeld has deigned to use its colorful futuristic furniture in his Monte Carlo apartment. At the moment perhaps the most prominent interior designer is Philippe Starck, who has produced new furnishings for the private apartments of the Elysée Palace. He recently renovated the interior of the Royalton Hotel in New York City, where he has reinterpreted some of the designs of the immediate past. Bold, clean lines of great elegance and ingenuity are his specialties. He came to prominence in 1978 with a canvas and metal chair called Dr. Bloodmoney. Light, cheap, and sloppily elegant, it had the sort of flea-market aura characteristic of the famous showcase apartment in Paris designed by Benjamin Baltimore, a graphics artist and film enthusiast. Part movie set and part art gallery, the *dernier-cri* interior, often used to illustrate the wave of the future, is a constantly changing mixture of found objects and construction materials. It is difficult, of course, to assess whether this avant-garde furniture will be a permanent part of design history.

The furniture of the twentieth century is made up of many threads and streams: the Arts and Crafts Movement, Art Nouveau, the Bauhaus, the Wiener Werkstätte, Art Deco, Scandinavian Modern, Italian Contemporary, and, of course, the memory of a thousand years of furniture design in western Europe. The styles of the past, as Hollis S. Baker learned early in his study of the long pageant of furniture, have all been expressions of contemporary life and the points of view of different civilizations with different imperatives.

Eames also created this lounge chair, a contemporary-looking piece that is also extremely comfortable. The same cannot be said of some other modern furniture.

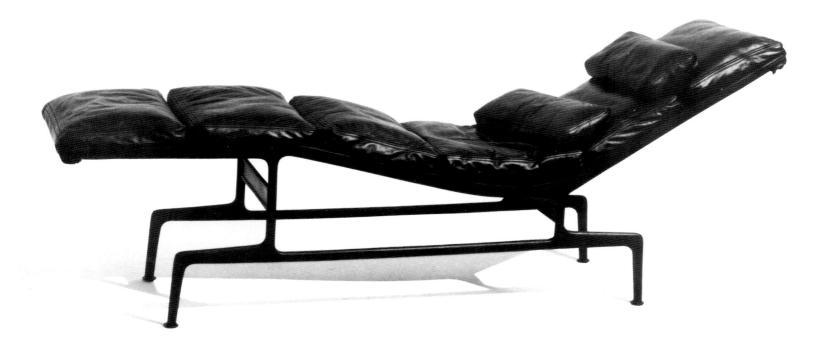

This tubular steel chair with no back legs is one of a variety of similar chairs designed by Ludwig Mies van der Rohe in 1930 for a glass-walled house in Brno, Czechoslovakia. Mies Van der Rohe said, "A chair is a very difficult object. A skyscraper is almost easier. That is why Chippendale is famous."

Simplicity itself is expressed in this handsome Alvar Aalto table from 1947, with laminated and bent wooden legs and a removable glass top.

Although Baker has made traditional
woodworking its principal occupation
during the first century of its
existence, some contemporary
collections have been very successful.
Here, Charles Pfister's dining-room
suite and bedroom pieces are at once
comfortable, pleasing to look at, and
functional.

In a contemporary setting, Charles
Pfister plays off the old-fashioned
sleigh bed in a modern form.

The Art of Reproduction

The Baker Furniture Company

The tradition of making reproduction furniture is a long and distinguished one. In the course of design history, there are perhaps three firms that stand out. One was a company in Paris belonging to Guillaume Grohé (1808–1885), a German-born French furniture maker during the Second Empire, originally an art dealer and furniture seller. By the 1860s he had moved to the reproduction of fine eighteenth-century French furniture, and his clients included both the French and English aristocracy of the day. Another master of the craft was the firm of Wassmus Frères, also operating in Paris during the era of Napoleon III. This company was known for its excellent reproductions of the work of André-Charles Boulle, principal *ébéniste* during the reign of Louis XIV. In England one of the most famous of all reproduction furniture makers was Gillows, founded by Robert Gillow in Lancaster, in 1731. The company was best known for its late-Georgian and Regency-style pieces, and it remained one of the most important British makers of reproduction furniture throughout the nineteenth century and well into the twentieth. About 1900 the firm merged with S.J. Waring & Sons to become Waring & Gillows, which remained in operation until 1974. Today the Baker Furniture Company joins the fine custom firms that have flourished in the long and elegant history of reproduction furniture.

Founded in Allegan, Michigan, Baker Furniture mirrors all the major developments in the American furniture industry and shows all those elements of entrepreneurship, innovation, and adaptability necessary to survival in any business. In miniature, it is the story of the American furniture industry from the earliest days of independent craftsmen and one-man cabinetmaking shops to the introduction of factory manufacturing processes in the mid-nineteenth century.

Cook, Baker & Co.   3

No. 85 Combination Bookcase
3 ft. 9 in. wide, 6 ft. 10 in. high. French bevel mirror 14x24. Made in quarter sawed oak and birch finished imitation mahogany. Has plate glass shelf in cabinet not shown in cut. An elegant case. Rubbed and polished.

Cook, Baker & Co.
Allegan, Mich.

MANUFACTURERS OF
Combination Bookcases, Libraries and Desks.
1897

Siebe Baker was born in Enkhuizen, the Netherlands, in 1852, and about 1870 he set out for the United States, where he found work as a builder and contractor. Within ten years he was operating Kolvoord & Baker, a successful general store in Hamilton, Michigan, and in 1890 he started the firm of Cook & Baker in Allegan, Michigan, with his friend Henry Cook, who was also born in the Netherlands. Together they bought a planing mill, a small wood-frame structure powered by water, that belonged to Nathan B. West. The plant was located in Allegan between the millrace and the river, and here the two Dutch craftsmen produced quality doors, sashes, and window blinds, along with general woodworking. In 1893 they made their first piece of furniture: a combination bookcase of the type so popular in those days, serving both as desk and bookcase. This was the Golden Oak era of American furniture (the palest yellow oak was popular in the Victorian years), and during the next decade buffets and china cabinets were added to the line. Today the Baker Furniture Museum in Holland, Michigan, contains a sample of the famous No. 96 bookcase, a simplified mix of Mission and Art Nouveau made in 1896 and sold at two for ten dollars, packed in a single crate. Cook & Baker was now firmly committed to the

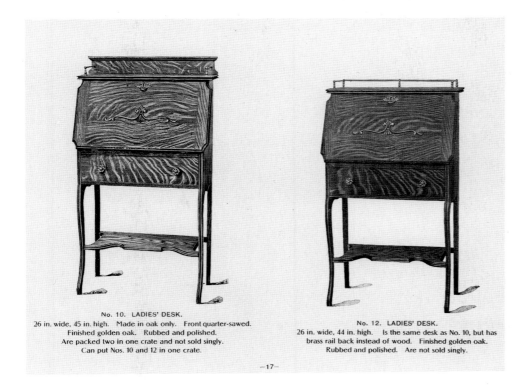

No. 10. LADIES' DESK.
26 in. wide, 45 in. high. Made in oak only. Front quarter-sawed.
Finished golden oak. Rubbed and polished.
Are packed two in one crate and not sold singly.
Can put Nos. 10 and 12 in one crate.

No. 12. LADIES' DESK.
26 in. wide, 44 in. high. Is the same desk as No. 10, but has
brass rail back instead of wood. Finished golden oak.
Rubbed and polished. Are not sold singly.

—17—

Early Baker catalogues featured golden oak furniture of modest design and reasonable cost.

furniture business, and in that same year of 1896 it was Allegan's leading employer with a payroll of thirty.

Product lines expanded steadily, and within ten years of the company's founding Cook & Baker was offering bookcases, desks, and other pieces for the home. In 1915 Siebe Baker became the firm's sole owner, and for the next three generations the Baker family built the company into one of the leaders of the American furniture industry. Almost from the beginning it was an active participant in the movement that made West Michigan an important center of furniture manufacturing. Industry-wide developments in design, manufacturing, technology, and marketing were almost always reflected by similar developments at Baker.

The importance of Dutch craftsmen and artisans in this area of West Michigan cannot be overestimated. In 1880 the editor of the *Grand Rapids Herald* humorously noted: "Grand Rapids has 10,000 population and 90,000 Dutch." And, in some remarks made in 1923, Mayor E.P. Stephan of Holland, Michigan, sung the praises of Dutch settlers in his part of the state: "Summed up, the message that Holland and Zeeland want to get across to all furniture dealers and ultimately to the consumer, is that 'If It's Made By Dutchmen, It's As Good As Can Be Made.'" Capital letters assured that no one missed the point.

Siebe Baker was a perfect example of what the mayor of Holland had in mind. He was not only a fine craftsman, but he had managed to turn himself into a shrewd businessman. As a matter of fact, shrewdness in business was another notable Dutch characteristic. Baker not only made timely changes in occupation to stay abreast of shifting conditions in nineteenth-century America (he had been variously a builder, a contractor, and a carpenter) but demonstrated remarkable flexibility in learning whatever new skills were demanded of him.

In 1903 the name of the firm was changed to Baker & Company, and it was incorporated in 1913. Over the years many additions were made to the plant. In 1910 Hollis S. Baker graduated from the University of Michigan and entered the business as a salesman. He advanced to the posts of secretary and treasurer in 1913, and upon the death of his father in 1925 became president. The first decade of his presidency marked an important period of development and expansion

By the 1930s Baker was already well on its way to offering a broad line of classic English eighteenth- and nineteenth-century reproductions.

of the company. Its name was changed to Baker Furniture Factories in 1927, and complete living room and bedroom lines were added to the inventory. Baker, being a student of the fine arts, had every intention of improving the line even more dramatically. His taste was sophisticated, and he had definite ideas about what he wanted to accomplish. He reorganized operations and produced exactly the sort of furniture *he* liked. Drive and vision and determination were characteristics he shared with his father. Paradoxically, much of the success he achieved can be

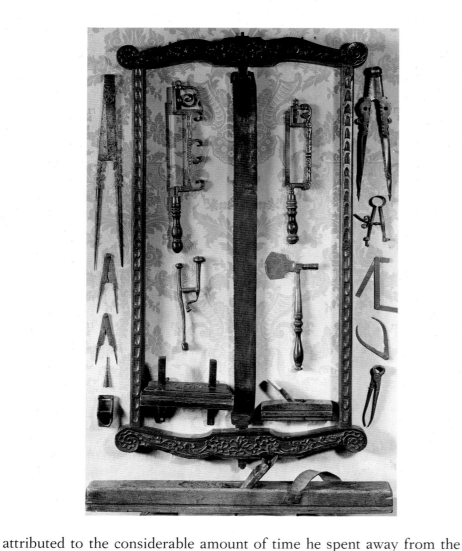

Displays at Baker's furniture museum near the company's plant in Holland, Michigan, include woodworker's tools, chairs, and other interesting and important examples of cabinetmaking.

attributed to the considerable amount of time he spent away from the company, traveling and researching abroad. Each year and sometimes twice a year he traveled to Europe, generally spending several months in England and France in search of the finest antique furniture. He gathered information everywhere—in museums, at auctions and private collections, in homes and shops. With a scholar's instinct he searched tirelessly for rare books and manuscripts concerned with the techniques and development of furniture in Western civilization. And regularly over the years, large shipments of his discoveries crossed the Atlantic on their way to Michigan, where they would go to the furniture factory or to the Baker Library or, in later years, to the Baker Furniture Museum. Incredibly, in addition to running a company that was growing larger and more profitable each year, he found time to gather material for a book about the history of furniture. However, with so many demands

on his time, Baker did not devote himself fully to his book until the last decade of his life. *Furniture in the Ancient World* was published in 1966, the year of his death.

In the course of Baker's research he needed some help to supplement his own efforts, so he commissioned Margaret Stephens Taylor, a professor at the Royal College of Art in London, to make measured drawings of antique furniture ordinarily seen only by collectors. Over the years hundreds of designs and drawings have found their way into company archives, even though many of them have never been produced. The drawings give accurate dimensions for each original and are carefully detailed, even to the point of reproducing the actual color of an unusual inlay or a rare wood.

Eventually much of the material found its way into the Baker Furniture Library, which is today one of the most complete interior design libraries in the country. A substantial number of volumes represent books and manuscripts that Baker collected in Europe and the United States over the course of some forty years. He acquired not only standard reference books about furniture and craftsmanship, but also many rare volumes long out of print. On one of his trips he acquired a

William Millington, Bakers first staff designer, made watercolor renderings of pieces to be introduced into the line. Millington had served his apprenticeship in a London cabinetmaker's shop founded in the eighteenth century.

collection of nearly two thousand photographs, detailed drawings, and plaster casts from one of England's oldest and most famous cabinetmaking shops, now out of existence. They represent a working record of more than fifty years of producing outstanding furniture.

The furniture of all styles and all eras that Baker collected both abroad and in the United States eventually formed the Baker Furniture Museum, established in the company showrooms in Grand Rapids,

Michigan, in 1941. Today it occupies its own building in Holland, Michigan, and contains splendid examples of antique furniture, ornamental details, and fragments for study and inspiration. All pieces are kept just as they were found, without benefit of repair, reconstruction, or refinishing. No attempt is made at decorative effect. Chairs stand in long rows; sofas, tables, chests, and desks are scattered about where they may be handled conveniently and looked at from every side. The museum contains the raw material of history, and as such it was a project of singular importance to Hollis S. Baker.

Indeed, by the beginning of the 1930s, he operated Baker Furniture under his own prescription that the company "will only make what I would buy myself." And his taste—as well as that of the general public—ran to the styles from eighteenth-century England and France, and to a lesser extent from Colonial and Federal America. In matters of design and finish all period pieces were authentic to the last detail. As early as 1923 Baker designers had visited a Duncan Phyfe exhibition at The Metropolitan Museum of Art in New York and designed a replica line. Baker consciously encouraged a policy that avoided presenting furniture that was in any way reminiscent of "standard Grand Rapids suites."

A tradition of fine reproductions was well under way. In 1929 the innovative concept of the Milling Road Shops was being developed, and it proved a retailing method remarkably wellsuited to the Baker product. The idea was created by William Millington (1879–1962), who joined Baker Furniture as head designer in 1927 and remained with the company until shortly before his death. Born in Lancaster, England, he had served a seven-year apprenticeship with the famous English firm of Waring & Gillows. By 1910 he had moved to New York, where he worked for W. & J. Sloan, and seven years later came to Grand Rapids, where he designed for a succession of furniture companies. At Baker Furniture he organized a set of reproduction rooms—a shop—that were available for stores like Wanamaker's and Bamberger's at a moderate cost. Each shop had a London storefront that Millington had copied at the Gyffre Museum, Shoreditch, from an original taken from 24 Northampton Street, Clerkenwell. The shop presented a special line of Baker Furniture products, designed for exclusive sale by a single dealer in that particular city, in each of its four rooms, a large one for showing living-room pieces and three smaller ones for bedroom, dining room, and library furniture. Baker Furniture provided architectural plans and supplied all moldings, paneling, and fireplaces, for the shop and the storefront itself.

The line featured reproductions of approximately sixty Georgian pieces that had been illustrated in *Connoisseur* magazine from 1900 to 1928, and from other English sources. The pieces were carefully finished to match the color and patina of the originals. In addition, each piece of furniture had a special descriptive and historical tag attached, such as: "Milling Road Shop/Copied from a desk owned by Owen Evan-Thomas at 20 Dover Street, London, England. Illustrated in May, 1928 issue of *Connoisseur*." Each was identified by number. Soon, some forty Milling Road shops existed nationwide.

Having established a reputation for historical integrity in his company's reproduction furniture, Hollis S. Baker then sought to establish the higher standards of craftsmanship. In 1932, he organized the Manor House, located in a four-story brownstone on East 67th Street in New York City. This separate company was established to produce and show exclusive lines of reproduction furniture. Since the

country was in the depths of the Great Depression, it was bold to start making the most expensive reproductions available anywhere in the United States. All pieces were made almost entirely by hand to the point of dovetailed drawer construction and hand finishing by craftsmen who had received their training in England, France, and Italy. These skilled cabinetmakers, working in a tradition handed down from Old World masters to sons and apprentices, were consummate perfectionists as they fitted joints or made certain drawers glided smoothly in solidly framed compartments. Later a number of these artisans were transferred to Holland, Michigan, and their skills have been handed down to later generations.

In the Manor House lay the seeds of Baker Furniture as it exists today, a company devoted to the making of fine reproduction furniture with a level of superior craftsmanship that, at one point, seemed destined to be lost forever. Hollis S. Baker's love of furniture led naturally to the great respect he always held for the craftsmen who were so necessary to the creation of the fine products he wanted to set before the public. Though many of the latest machines available for the

manufacture of furniture are used in Baker's plants today, the emphasis is still—as it was in 1932—on handwork and the individual craftsman.

Over the years the company has presented many lines of authentic reproductions from some of the richest historical periods in furniture history, ranging from the Old World Collection of 1931 to the Stately Homes Collection of 1981. In 1949 there was the Far East Collection, adaptations of antique pieces from China and Korea and other Asian countries. The finest teak and walnut were used, and every detail followed original designs with authentic pewter and brass hardware.

Palladian appeared in 1950, the name derived from the sixteenth-century Italian architect Andrea Palladio. To create this line Baker designers studied, measured, and photographed museum originals and brought back many pieces that are now in the Baker Furniture Museum. In 1954 the company presented Continental, a sampling of eighteenth- and nineteenth-century Italian, English Regency, and Austrian Biedermeier pieces. The woods used were as authentic as the designs; Baker craftsmen used local European woods whenever possible, particularly walnut and cherry, and finished them beautifully. All hardware was specially designed, based on European originals and in some cases made in Italy to Baker specifications. The list continues: Britannia in 1966; Normandy, shown at the Chicago Furniture Fair of 1967, a splendid example of the French provincial style, quite different from the elaborate ormolu-laden furniture of the Louis XV and Louis XVI periods. There was handsome carving, rugged hardware, and carefully aged woods such as cherry, French oak, and walnut. The pieces were reproduced from originals in the Baker Furniture Museum and involved extensive research by designers and craftsmen in all departments.

Woburn Abbey appeared in 1969: a selection of approximately twenty-five reproductions of eighteenth-century English furniture from the home of the duke of Bedford. Each piece was personally selected by the duke and Hollis M. Baker, president of the company at the time. The grandson of Siebe Baker noted in the catalogue for the collection: "For the three generations in which the Baker family has been steeped in the tradition of fine furniture—as an absorbing hobby as well as a business—our search for new sources of design inspiration has led us to many countries and through many private collections. . . . In the fullest sense, our Woburn Abbey Collection reaffirms our pledge and policy: To make furniture that will be worthy of those who appreciate the finest." In general, the selection process demonstrated the underlying philosophy of the company regarding the reproduction of antique furniture: it must represent the highest standards of traditional design and craftsmanship; it must be suitable for home use; and it must have some characteristic that makes it outstanding on its own. Margaret Stephens Taylor of London's Royal College of Art made measured

Pride in craftsmanship has long been a Baker quality. These publicity photographs, made in the 1930s, introduced skilled Baker workers—glazing, carving, and assembling various pieces—to magazine audiences.

drawings of all the furniture to be reproduced, and each drawing recorded the most minute details of line and dimension.

An impressive advance in the refinement and sophistication of this approach is to be found in the Stately Homes Collection presented in 1981. Sir Humphrey Wakefield, Bt., a renowned authority on the history and development of furniture with an unsurpassed knowledge of Great Britain's private collections, made the selections and wrote a brief history of each stately home for the catalogue. He explains: "In the 18th century the all too powerful aristocratic owners of Stately Homes commissioned the greatest furniture in that remarkable era of creation. Whatever those 18th century leaders of fashion and power ordained was then dutifully copied for the general public—well or badly according to the artistry of the craftsmen!" Sir Humphrey found the approach of Baker enviable: "The Baker Furniture Company has devoted hand craftsmen who carve and recarve till a line suddenly picks up a dynamic harmonic from the original—and then colour and recolour till the tones blend and meld with those of two centuries ago. These craftsmen have a more complex task than their forebears, as Nature's all too subtle hallmark of gentle wear, and dappled sunbleaching, has to be suggested and intriguingly involved to calm the connoisseur's eye."

All of the pieces chosen are intriguing, as are the brief descriptions of the families who owned them and the castles or country houses in which they had been found. Here are, in the words of the catalogue, "exacting reproductions of superb antiques, each piece the prized treasure of a nobleman and still housed in a great Stately Home." These range from Barons Court in County Tyrone, Ireland, the home of the duke of Abercorn, to Blenheim Palace in Oxfordshire, England, the home of the duke of Marlborough. There are splendid pieces from famous homes like Burghley House, Chatsworth House, Floors Castle, Cliveden Place, Newstead Abbey, Penshurst Place, and Stratfield Saye House, the home of the duke of Wellington.

One of the richest of the private collections made available to Baker customers was contained at Longleat House in Wiltshire, the home of the marquess of Bath and one of the most impressive concentrations of Georgian furniture in the British Isles. Longleat was built in 1554, a great house surrounded by magnificent grounds set out

This original watercolor rendering from 1951 by Finn Juhl, the Danish architect/designer, served as a working plan for Baker craftsmen in reproducing one of several Juhl pieces.

Baker's earliest connection with England's great country houses was Woburn Abbey, north of London. The original of this handsome bookcase belonged to the duke of Bedford.

This butler's table, with ingenious folding wings that triple its surface area, has been in continuous production at Baker since the 1930s, a remarkable life for an object in a business that is, after all, subject to changing fashions.

In 1961 designer T.H. Robsjohn-Gibbings offered a living room suite of cool classicism. The side chair at the right echoes the Greek klismos *chair of antiquity.*

in the eighteenth century by the landscape architect Lancelot "Capability" Brown. The collection illustrates five hundred years worth of art and furniture of all kinds, but many notable examples of fine eighteenth-century furniture inspired the craftsmen at Baker: two Chippendale sofas and a partners' desk; a George I tub chair and George III satinwood and parquetry pedestal table; a carved mahogany architect's table. In the library is a lovely Regency fiddleback mahogany writing table, its rectangular top inset with a tooled leather panel and its drawers inlaid with an ebonized key pattern and geometric bands. There is also a magnificent Chippendale mahogany double serpentine partners' pedestal desk, from about 1760. Another remarkable piece is the George I walnut tub chair, with cabriole legs and classic pad feet, about 1718. All of these pieces, and the dozens like them, have been duplicated by Baker Furniture as perfectly as possible and, whenever feasible, using the hand skills of the eighteenth century.

By 1988 Baker was engaged in creating an even more extensive and sophisticated collection of reproduction furniture in collaboration with the New York interior design firm McMillen, Inc. For over sixty-five years the firm has created outstanding traditional interior design,

A Baker showroom in the mid-1970s displayed a variety of wood and upholstered pieces.

and the McMillen Collection now presented by Baker includes reproductions of pieces collected not only by McMillen itself but by some of its many clients. The result is a collection far more eclectic and encompassing than anything Baker Furniture has ever attempted to produce at one time. There are, for example, exquisite pieces in eighteenth- and nineteenth-century French, Italian, English, Dutch, American, and Chinese designs. In each instance, everything has been reproduced by Baker craftsmen down to the last detail; they have re-created the handsomely figured woods, finely decorated lacquers, antique paint finishes, and detailed upholstery. Indeed, the collection represents a brilliant *tour de force* for Baker, and all the skills of furniture reproduction have been shown to the public at one time in this line. One of the most striking pieces reproduced is an elaborately lacquered Venetian secretary, dating from the eighteenth century. The collection is compelling evidence that Baker is moving rapidly and firmly in the direction of complete home furnishings and that the company is making a design statement concerned not only with individual pieces of furniture from the past, but with fabrics and decorative accessories of all kinds.

Materials and Techniques

It must be remembered that furniture classified as antique is not automatically of good quality. Badly constructed pieces have been made in every era in history. "Schlock" and "Borax" are terms used in the furniture industry to describe badly made furniture of any period or date, and they have helped destroy the myth that things were better in the old days. The creation of a piece of finished furniture, like the creation of a fine painting or sculpture, depends on a close relationship between the artist-craftsman and the materials with which he works. The final excellence of the product involves choice woods, along with the meticulous attention of cabinetmakers, carvers, and finishers who have devoted a lifetime to the mastery of their craft.

Vital to the cabinetmaker's art is the quality and figure, or surface design, of the wood itself. Wood holds a fascination that few other basic materials have. Mankind's oldest resource, it has provided fuel, tools, light, and shelter through thousands of years of civilization. Fortunately, it is also a resource that nature can renew. Because selection of the right wood is so basic to making fine furniture, Baker Furniture scouts search continually throughout the world for those trees to which time, soil, and weather conditions have imparted a special, sometimes even a spectacular, beauty. Species such as French oak, *merisier* (French white cherry), European and Persian walnut, Brazilian rosewood, East Indian satinwood, and Burmese teak, as well as the finest examples of mahogany, are carefully selected in the countries in which they grow.

The importance of wood cannot be overstated. It would be impossible to reproduce a Biedermeier chest, for example, with its typical honey-colored glow, without the burl veneer from elms that grow in the Carpathian Mountains of Eastern Europe or veneers from one of the fruitwoods—apple, cherry, or pear—native to the area where European cabinetmakers of the past chose their materials. It would be impossible to re-create one of those scrubbed-looking French Provincial armoires unless one had hard-surfaced, pinstripe French oak veneer to work with; or to reproduce a Louis XVI chest without *merisier*. Nor would it be possible to reproduce a Queen Anne chest without veneers from a particular species of walnut that was originally exported from Persia to Italy and then on to England during the Roman conquest of that country. It would be equally impossible to reproduce an English Welsh dresser without pollard-oak veneer, its extraordinary graining achieved by cutting back the top branches (or crown) to the trunk in order to stimulate the growth of new shoots and give the matured wood a unique character and a compelling figure.

Even in the twentieth century, for all the popularity of metal and plastic, wood is still the most important and widely used material in furniture making. It is essential that the cabinetmaker have a genuine understanding of wood, its characteristics and various manifestations. It is not as easy to recognize wood as one might think. The effects of sunlight, for example, can make such different woods as mahogany, walnut, and cherry look remarkably alike, and it must be remembered that cheap soft woods like pine can be stained to look like rosewood, cherry, or maple. Certain woods have been favorites of the finest cabinetmakers of the past and, it might be added, of the present. Ebony, for example, is highly prized because of its dense black color. For two hundred years mahogany has formed the finest antique furniture, and it is one of the glories of eighteenth-century English and American furniture. With its rich color and handsome figure it makes the ideal cabinet material—strong and resistant to warping and decay. There are three main types: Spanish mahogany, the ideal being from Santo Domingo, dark and straight-grained but no longer available; Cuban mahogany, now equally rare, with a far more elaborate figure; and Central American mahogany. Today, Central American mahogany is regularly used. It is softer than Spanish mahogany, more orange in color, and often has interesting figures. Antique pieces made of it are often heavily scratched and dented. By the end of the nineteenth century dwindling supplies of true mahogany led to the use of similar woods like African mahogany, which is lighter, less attractively marked, and not as strong as Central American mahogany. In addition, there are many rare and exotic woods used in the making of antique furniture (and, required for the duplication of it): Brazilian rosewood, West Indian satinwood, tulipwood. Walnut, too, is considered one of the best woods for cabinetmaking. It is fairly hard but easy to work and is usually

Paying homage to historic Charleston came naturally to Baker, since that southern coastal city had been an important center for the production of fine English-influenced, early American furniture. During a relatively short period in its early history when Charleston was larger and richer than either New York or Boston, the city supported some 250 independent cabinetmakers.

In 1987 Baker introduced a new line called French À La Carte, based largely on rural designs created by cabinetmakers from the provinces.

marked with a varied figure that is difficult to match in other woods.

The conversion of carefully selected woods into fine furniture begins in the drying kilns where planks are slowly seasoned to remove moisture and to insure against later warping or splitting. They are then rough-formed by modern machine tools because, as with the shaping of a piece of sculpture, initial cuts simply trim away the excess and have little to do with the final artistry. The use of twentieth-century technology results in significant savings in time and cost, but many painstaking hand techniques from the past are regularly used at the Baker Furniture Company.

Working with veneer is one of the most important skills involved in the reproduction of antique furniture. Veneer is a thin sheet of fine wood attached to an underlying layer of less expensive material. (Today particleboard of great strength and rigidity is used for a completely flat surface since, unlike wood, it has no tendency to move or expand.) When making sheets of veneer from a log, different methods of cutting will produce different figures that are the basic attraction of veneer. Depending upon the part of the tree they come from, different sheets of wood will bear distinctive figures, such as in burl and oyster veneers. Sheets from the same piece of wood bear the same figuring, and these matching sheets may be halved or quartered and the pieces arranged in striking configurations to make "a book," since the sheets of wood are indeed arranged side by side like the pages of a book to create the most interesting and beautiful design possible. As T.P. Yardley, executive vice president of Baker Furniture today, explains: "Everything beautiful is the result of a struggle." In the finest figuring, like that found in crotch mahogany, the limbs of the tree have struggled in opposite directions and created fascinating and provocative figures. The veneer craftsman must select, match, and cut the sheets of veneer—some of them as rare and fragile as fine old lace—and fit them, with exquisite precision, to each assembled piece.

At Baker, the gathering of fine veneers from sources in Europe and South America and their eventual arrival in the loading docks at the Holland or Grand Rapids plants are often involved and expensive operations. The best bird's-eye maple, for example, is grown in northern Michigan, not that far from the Baker factories, but it is cut to veneer width in Switzerland and dyed in Italy and *then* returned to Holland and Grand Rapids. A rare and lovely wood like tulipwood comes from South America a whole tree at a time, sliced into .44-inch thickness and wrapped in coarse boards and bound with iron baling straps.

In the Baker Furniture factories there are no assembly lines as such, but at every step of the way a different sort of handcraftman is required. In breakfronts or secretaries, English crown glass is used in the doors. This hand-blown glass is made in England by just one firm, following two-hundred-year-old methods. Its slightly convex surface and faint whorls give it the texture and brilliance of fine antique glass. There are the arts of lacquering (what was called "japanning" in the eighteenth century) and gilding and all the handwork that cannot ever be done by machines and ultimately makes exquisite reproductions possible. Older techniques of lacquering involved using sap from the *lac* tree (grown in China and Japan), dissolving it in rectified alcohol, and spreading it on the piece in thin coats. The piece was painstakingly polished after each coat dried. Much of this laborious process is unnecessary today; there are splendid lacquers made from synthetic materials derived from cellulose. Marquetry and intarsia also represent special skills where ivory, ebony, brass, gold wire, mother-of-pearl, and antique gold and silver gilding are often used in the most elaborate furniture today. Eighteenth-century furniture in particular relies for its decorative effects on a good deal of elaborate marquetry and intarsia. Marquetry is the extensive use of inlaid veneers from many different woods to create handsome pictorial designs. Intarsia is a similar process, although by contrast it uses small pieces of inlaid wood to create abstract and architectural designs. It was particularly popular during the Italian Renaissance.

The final step and one of the most important in the process of making reproductions is hand polishing, which produces a soft, glowing patina. The talents of the finisher cannot be overestimated. In order to catch all the subtle nuances of antique furniture, an expert finisher must be an artist in a very real sense of the word. In fact, his materials and tools do resemble those of a fine artist at work on a painting. As does the master of fine art, the finisher uses whatever colors and toning are necessary to create the desired finished effect. There is no set formula,

and each piece is an individual creation. In the past, Baker often found it necessary to recruit such specialists from small custom shops in England, France, and Italy or in the small shops found in the lofts of New York during the early 1930s. However, Baker soon perfected a form of French polishing that marked an important development in the manufacturing of fine reproduction furniture in the United States. The Baker finish produced a result completely different from the harsh precision and shiny surfaces then common in so-called "Grand Rapids" furniture. It was not applied with brush or spray; instead it was worked into the wood by hand with a small pad. This is one of those important hand techniques for which there is no machine substitute. French polish contained shellac with various hardeners and gums added to a base of alcohol or industrial spirits. Historically, the earliest finishes for wood

Baker created numerous handsome room settings to show the Stately Homes Collection pieces for magazine and trade journal advertising.

The Northern Italian Collection, introduced in 1988, featured a number of painted pieces (far left) in keeping with the style of the region. Baker's designers, working from originals purchased abroad, sometimes modified proportions or details in order to make them more suitable for contemporary American living. The small Rococo dining room server, shown at left, was made available in both a painted and a wood finish. The dining table seen on the following page offered bold carving.

were either simple waxes or an oil varnish made by dissolving copal resin into linseed or poppy oil. By the middle of the seventeenth century shellac made by dissolving lac in spirits of wine became popular. The true technique of French polishing appeared in the 1820s, gradually replacing other finishes. The polishing pad is made by taking a piece of absorbent cotton and folding it into a firm egg shape. A pointed end and a blunted end are made, and finally the pad is wrapped in linen. French polishing has always been considered a separate craft, indeed an art of its own. It results in a mirror finish and requires an

For a more contemporary look in the
1980s, Baker featured a modular
system of bird's-eye maple designed by
Bryan Palmer.

extraordinary amount of time to accomplish. Nevertheless, the technique was used at Baker Furniture well into the 1930s, but today it has been replaced by synthetic lacquers, which are much more durable, not as unstable as shellac, and produce a more even finish than the old painstaking French polishing.

Hardware such as brass pulls and ornaments must also receive meticulous attention in the art of fine furniture reproduction. Indeed, they were often reproduced in Europe from the same antique molds that artisans of bygone years had used. Other skills are increasingly in demand, and today the craft of upholstery plays an increasingly important role in the making of Baker reproductions. In the basic sense upholstery has been used for chairs and couches since Egyptian times when material—reed, animal skins, cloth—was stretched across a rigid frame and loose pillows were scattered on the piece. By the sixteenth century padding and cushions were joined together, covered by material and tacked to a frame. After the development of metal springs the upholstery of furniture as we know it today began, and Baker uses the

In the early 1980s Alessandro created a stunning collection for Baker, featuring a variety of complex shapes (challenging the cabinetmakers) as well as more than two dozen faux finishes imitating marble, other stones, and rare woods.

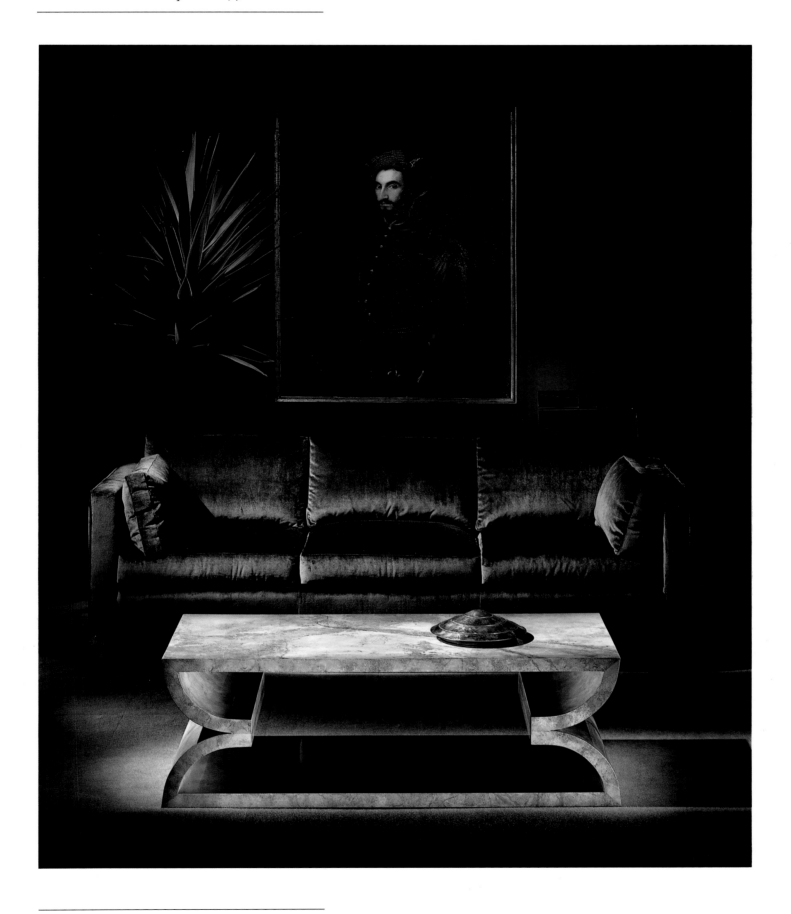

New York interior designer John Saladino created these sophisticated ensembles for Baker in 1985.

most modern techniques. Comfortable upholstery is one of the most important of the furniture-making crafts. Since so much of it is hidden, it is important to have confidence in the integrity of the maker, since even today there is no standardization of quality.

One of the master carvers familiar with every aspect of craftsmanship at Baker Furniture is Lloyd Van Doornik, who joined the company over forty years ago as a young apprentice. It has been his job to create a prototype model for every important piece of furniture decoration: a Chippendale leg, an elaborate fretwork, a delicate frieze. The master carver, in fact, is one of the chief artisans on the factory floor. On his bench are tools that have seen service for two lifetimes: over three hundred antique tools, many of them collected in Europe over fifty years ago. The tradition of the craftsman is preserved today at Baker as it is in few other places in the United States or in Europe, for that matter. And it is found in few mass production furniture enterprises anywhere in the world. Staining wood, for example, is entrusted to colorists, many of whom have also been with the company for over forty years. And the leather craftsman says that the dyes, or leather marking tools, hanging on the wall behind him were there when he arrived some forty years ago. They were among the many treasures that Hollis S. Baker sent back almost yearly to Holland, Michigan, after his trips abroad in the 1930s.

All the work, knowledge, skill, and research that go into the reproduction of fine furniture do not, of course, guarantee a fine product. The only thing that can guarantee the product is a good eye. Styles can be learned from textbooks, but appreciation of the intricacies of design requires the constant examination and analysis of innumerable pieces of furniture. This is the principle to which Hollis S. Baker devoted his entire career and which was maintained by his son when he became president of the company.

"For three generations, the Baker family has been steeped in the traditions of making fine furniture," explains Hollis M. Baker, grandson of Siebe Baker. "Our study and research and our efforts to find ways of re-creating the techniques of the great furniture craftsmen of the past are all directed to the production of a finished product worthy of our motto, 'For those who appreciate the finest.'"

The Factory Floor

Before the 1930s the main sources for fine furniture reproductions were small cabinetmaking shops in England, France, and, to a lesser extent, in the United States. The cost of the work involved was beyond the means of most people. These small workshops were in the habit of making only one or two copies of an antique piece, and the average customer was hardly being served in any significant way. It was Hollis S. Baker's feeling that a significant number of reproductions could be made at the same time on mass production principles with the same care and results as the production of one or two pieces. Thus today fifty cuttings of one design are generally produced and, in the case of more popular pieces, one hundred. Often pieces are left "in the white" (unfinished) until special orders can be filled. Nevertheless, whenever possible, modern techniques are used to cut down on the amount of

Above, left: Master carver Lloyd Van Doornik, using tools of the past and with hands trained by more than forty–three years of Baker experience, sculpts the leg of a Regency console table. Some mechanical means are employed to copy a particular part, but hand finishing by other carvers always follows. Above: A specialist in veneers, Alice Weller matches grains and tapes together pieces of rosewood to form the intricate pattern of an English Regency dining-table top.

handwork required. Without compromising the finished product, the craftsmen at Baker found that they could create a fine piece of furniture by maintaining a delicate balance between mass production and one-of-a-kind cabinetmaking. On the factory floor, wherever possible, the principles of mass production and the assembly line are used, and the machine is substituted for handwork as long as the reproduction piece is in no way compromised.

Frank Edward Ransom, historian of the Grand Rapids furniture industry, explains the delicate balance that must be maintained: "Increasing use of machinery has eliminated much of the handwork in making even the finest furniture, but in certain phases of manufacture no satisfactory substitute for hand labor has been found. Although the major portion of the carving is accomplished by machine, carvers are still needed to create the master patterns. In the finishing . . . when as many as twenty-one operations may take place, machinery is used even

Above: Glazier Homer Louks takes responsibility for installing English Crown glass in breakfronts, secretaries, and display cabinets. Above, right: For more than twenty years, Susan Boerigter has brought the rich color of historic antiques to immaculately sanded and prepared new wood, using a variety of traditional stains and modern finishes to enhance the natural grain.

more sparingly. Staining and drying may be accomplished with the aid of machines, but hand sanding at this stage has no mechanical rival. . . . Overtoning, the blending of adjoining pieces of wood, is a hand operation. . . . The secret of a superb finish is justly said to be a little polish and 'a lot of elbow grease.'" In other words, you hardly need hordes of workers pouring in and out of forty-acre buildings.

From a technical point of view furniture today is actually far better than it was in the past. Every significant modern advance has been incorporated into the Baker factories. New glues are used everywhere, for example, and they are far more effective than the old animal glues (used, however, until well into the 1930s at Baker Furniture). In fact, it must be said that the greatest advances of all in the furniture industry have been made in the area of adhesives and in the new synthetic lacquer finishes, far more durable than the shellac of the old French polishing method. The idea at Baker is to use as much machinery and new technology as possible, as long as it offers a genuine improvement in the finished product or speed of operation or improves the looks or the strength of a piece of furniture. Some of the machinery is awesome: a huge German carving machine (which works rather like duplicating a key); a miraculous CNC router, a computer-controlled cutting and channeling machine developed within the last ten years that assures perfect reproduction every time; a laser cutter for fretwork, again computer operated and requiring sophisticated software. Machine sanding between coats of lacquer can be more effective and produce a more even finish on large surfaces. In general, the machine is used sparingly, since handwork forms much of the mystique of Baker. Every piece is different: "We fight uniformity on all sides," says T.P. Yardley.

Handwork, along with the application of assembly-line methods, can be seen in the progress of one classic Chippendale-style chair through the manufacturing process. The famous No. 789 chair was first made in 1932 from Cuban mahogany—it sold then for $16.95—and production of it has never stopped. In many ways it is similar to another chair found on one of the trips that Hollis S. Baker constantly took to England and other parts of Europe, during which he discovered the original of an important Chippendale chair in the village of High Wycombe, some twenty-six miles north of London. In the village was one of the choicest private collections of chairs in England. Although the piece was not for sale, permission was given Baker to have a cabinetmaker fashion an exact copy.

A fine Chippendale chair is one of the most difficult of all pieces to reproduce with complete fidelity. It has many compound curves and other matters of cabinetwork and carving that are almost impossible to put on paper. For these reasons the Baker Company has established a policy not to depend on drawings or photographs in the making of fine reproductions. It is important to remember that furniture is a three-dimensional art form, so every detail of this chair was copied, and the color and all aspects of the carving were duplicated exactly.

Once the piece, whatever its provenance, arrives in Holland, Michigan, it is turned over to the designer. It may seem unnecessary to have a designer when the original piece is present, but he plays an important role in the re-creation of a fine original. He is the keystone of the structure. Upon his shoulders rests the responsibility for translating the original into the drawings and details from which carvers and cabinetmakers work. The company is fortunate in having had many great designers in the past, men like William Millington, Frank VanSteenberg, Herbert Ten Have, and others. It is the designer's responsibility to break the design into its component parts, putting them in pattern form on a wooden "rod," a sheet of plywood five feet long and twenty-five inches wide, though the paper blueprint is more often used today as a guide for craftsmen. In ways that only thirty or forty years of experience can guarantee, Baker cabinetmakers duplicate all the intangible characteristics of the original. Sometimes, plaster casts of special features are made as well.

This is the preparatory work necessary to the reproduction of an original like the No. 789 Chippendale chair. Next comes the work of the cabinetmakers. The transformation is almost magical. When the chair enters the cabinet room, the back simply has a heavy slab of mahogany for the center, securely joined by the cabinetmaker into two strong pieces, selected for texture, that will form the legs. The back is cut out roughly and then sent to the hand carver. Constantly referring to the original, the carver repeats its character in the reproduction. Each leaf and detail of the original piece is reproduced by skillful carving, so that

Harold Kuiper, whose name echoes the Dutch origins of many craftsmen in Baker's Holland and Zeeland, Michigan, workshops, applies a gold-leaf bead to a leather-topped card table from the Stately Homes Collection.

Decorating supervisor in Baker's large studio, Arloa Perez meticulously re-creates painted patterns of a wide variety of traditional designs from ancient China to rural Italy. Here she works on the footboard of a Victorian-period bed from the McMillen Collection.

what was once a large plank is now transformed into the elaborately shaped back of the chair.

Then the finish: Graceful form and fine carvings are lacquered to give the added beauty that time and countless polishings brought to the original. This is the province of the finisher. The finish developed by Baker is now considered a standard in the high end of the American furniture industry.

The last stage in the manufacture of the chair is the upholstery. The best grade of webbing is used to support fine oil-tempered springs. After the strings are tied properly, they are surmounted with a layer of selected tail and mane hair which in turn is covered with fine cotton and muslin. The final cover is then applied by a skilled upholsterer. The procedure followed in making the No. 789 is comparable to that which is used for each piece in the extensive Baker repertoire of reproduction furniture, although some pieces require less carving and more inlay, or less shaping of wood and more tailoring in the upholstery.

The care and cost involved in the making of fine reproduction furniture may seem to rival the expense of an antique, but each year it becomes more difficult to acquire authentic antiques of any kind. Consider two recent sales of rare pieces: In the fall of 1988, at the *Biennale des Antiquaires* show in Paris, a small eighteenth-century *secrétaire* (roughly three and a half feet tall) sold for some five million dollars. Why was this little desk so valuable? It is the only surviving piece of period French furniture with mauve porcelain plaques, highly fashionable just before the French Revolution. It was made in 1778 by the Paris cabinetmaker Martin Carlin, whose specialty was to add Sèvres plaques—in this case, eleven of them. The small amounts of wood base still visible through all the ormolu are mahogany and tulipwood veneer. How did the piece survive the French Revolution? All we know is that it appeared in Baron Alphonse de Rothschild's collection in the 1800s.

A Goddard-Townsend six-shell blockfront secretary (a mahogany desk and bookcase combined), attributed to the shop of the legendary Rhode Island cabinetmaker John Goddard, is another example. It is one of ten known secretaries made between 1760 and 1775 in the Newport shop. Sam Pennington, editor of the *Maine Antique Digest*, said: "I

suspect there's going to be blood on the floor at Christie's." Perhaps
there was, for the piece was sold in the summer of 1989 for eleven
million dollars, an almost unbelievable sum.

These are perhaps the ultimate in antique furniture sales, but they
surely show the dilemma facing the consumer who wants beautiful and
historical pieces. There is, however, a solution for this public, the very
same middle-class public that caused the "democratization" of furniture
in the eighteenth century. Objects of beauty, taste, and fine
workmanship are still expensive, but not unrealistic, as antiques have
become. The Baker Furniture Company has found a welcome niche
between the world of unaffordable and unavailable antiques on one side
and the world of cheap reproductions on the other.

New Directions

Over the course of a hundred years, the integrity of product has been
miraculously maintained at the Baker Furniture Company. By the same
token the integrity and individuality of the company itself have been
maintained in the face of mergers and ownership by larger companies.
This is due to the executives who have consistently supported the
company. In so many businesses in the United States there is a gulf
between the creative and executive level, but this has never been the
case at Baker. The reason stems from the founder himself and from his
son, Hollis S. Baker, and his grandson, Hollis M. Baker. There is no
doubt that their sympathies were with the craftsman and the artisan.
Siebe Baker, after all, *was* a craftsman.

Loyalty, of course, is one of the great characteristics of the
executives and craftsmen of Baker and of all the people who have been
concerned with the success of the company. The areas of advertising
and public relations, for example, have been handled for almost fifty
years by Aves Advertising of Grand Rapids, a firm founded by Wesley
Aves in 1943 and today managed by his son, John C. Aves. Wesley
Aves, it must be pointed out, had been the manager of Baker's first
showroom in New York in the 1930s. This is simply another example of
the company's appealing sense of tradition and continuity.

These feelings have survived today on the factory floors at Holland and Grand Rapids. Furniture moves at a stately pace from one process to the next, from one skilled craftsman to the next. There are quotas, to be sure, and there are time-flow charts, but the ultimate decisions rest with the master craftsmen.

After 1969, when Hollis M. Baker sold the company to Magnavox and no one with the Baker name was left, a series of strong executives succeeded in maintaining the independence and integrity of the company in the face of mergers with larger entities: Magnavox, North American Phillips, and, today, the Kohler Company.

T.P. Yardley and Frank VanSteenberg, Sr. were the first of these executives, both furniture men with long experience in the company. "We've had a philosophy, and we've always set out deliberately to see how much handwork was justifiable," said VanSteenberg, who entered the factory as an apprentice in 1927 and went on to become a designer. "I believe apprenticeship is the only way. Fortunately there are more young people interested today in being trained in the crafts. . . . To us a chair leg is a piece of sculpture, each one is different. There's a lot of satisfaction in making something like this, no question about it." He went on to explain the techniques: "It's all a matter of touch and feel. Every detail is gone over by hand. One door may go through 250 different points in its making, from veneering to sanding to coloring." VanSteenberg was associated with Baker for more than fifty years. From 1953 to 1961 he was president of the company, and director from 1961 to 1975. He was the principal architect of the merger between Baker and Knapp & Tubbs, and his contributions cannot be exaggerated.

In 1975 Philip E. Kelley became president after the merger with Knapp & Tubbs, of which he had been president, in 1972. He is responsible for many innovative and aggressive marketing moves: showroom expansion, arranging for the company to be the first tenant at the Pacific Design Center in Los Angeles, and setting the stage for designer showrooms all over the country. Incidentally, Kelley acknowledges the inspiration for the gallery concept (now commonplace in the industry), which he received from Hollis S. Baker's similar move with the Manor House in 1932. "A national showroom network has made Baker, Knapp & Tubbs unique, and it started the gallery concept in retailing," explains Kelley. What Kelley accomplished were the sort of things Hollis S. Baker would have done himself: arrangements by architect and designer Brian Palmer, a stunning collection of modular furniture in bird's-eye maple that sold for as much as thirty-five thousand dollars a wall; the daring Alessandro Collection in marble and goatskin and other exotic materials; the successful Historic Charleston Collection, indeed the first really successful line of American reproductions in the country; the doubling of the volume of manufacturing space and the use of factories in North Carolina, particularly the Magnavox cabinet plant in Andrews; the purchase of Mastercraft; the opening of Baker's first upholstery factory in High Point, North Carolina; and, perhaps most important, the introduction of the Stately Homes Collection in 1981.

Robert Fernbacher, who became president in 1983, concentrated on fabrics and upholstery and the sort of quality that often demands ten or twelve silkscreenings. He led the company into a wider area of style and interior design. He sees more than simply furniture and has added color, style, and accessories by concentrating on the network of retailers that the Knapp & Tubbs showrooms provided. He made the company a style leader in the industry with the Stately Homes Collection, in which he, Philip Kelley, and others were involved. His development of the Charles Pfister contemporary collection and, most importantly, the McMillen Collection had an even more sophisticated and a broader impact. He succeeded in leading Baker into a commanding position of leadership in the high-end furniture industry of the United States. The company exceeds industry standards for both rate and profitability.

And today, Rod Kreitzer, the new president, is prepared to lead the company toward the twenty-first century. "The search for fine antiques, and Baker's painstaking care in reproducing them, is more than just a business," says Kreitzer. "Good design affects all of us today, perhaps more extensively than ever before. In every aspect of our environment —in the clothes we wear, in the objects we use, in the home furnishings with which we live—good design plays a major role that influences our comfort and our enjoyment of life.

"Today, Baker Furniture is fully committed to maintaining its hundred-year heritage of design and craftsmanship. We accept the responsibility and challenge of a splendid history, and we will make every effort to enhance and further that history."

Baker has become a big business in a way it never was when it was a Baker family company, particularly after its acquisition by Kohler Company in 1986 and the leadership of Herbert V. Kohler. In a curious way, however, its individualistic point of view has survived through all the corridors of big business. All the executives who have run the company after 1969 are entirely different from one another, but they all share a belief in the quality and independence, the honesty and integrity of Baker Furniture. In this they shared the same *esprit de corps* that can be seen everywhere on the factory floors, where a hundred-year-old tradition and centuries-old skills have combined.

There is a remarkable calm and quiet on the factory floors in Holland and Grand Rapids. A slight mist of sawdust hangs in the air, and here and there is the noise of some large and impressive (often German or Swiss) machine, but mostly one notices the quiet figure of a craftsman surrounded by one or two pieces waiting on the assembly line for the application of his particular expertise. It is almost precisely the way furniture has been made for two hundred years—though the modern world has scarcely been ignored.

In 1955 Frank Edward Ransom, historian of the Grand Rapids furniture industry, said: "Today, as throughout its history, the furniture industry of Grand Rapids is characterized by small units, individual rather than large corporate entrepreneurship, quality products, and individualistic workmen." Nothing has changed. It is a business where close enough is never good enough, where the product is considered as obsessively by the executive in his office as by the apprentice on the factory floor, or the master carver at his tool rack.

Retired Baker furniture designer Herbert Ten Have, with his reassuring Dutch name that echoes both the creative history of the company and the heritage of Grand Rapids, may be entitled to the last word. "Wood is ambiguous," he says. "It is hard, but there is something soft about it, too. You can look into a beautiful piece of polished wood to almost any depth you want—and see almost anything you want to see." Surely some of this magic will accompany the Baker Furniture company into its second hundred years.

In 1990, Baker's centennial year, one of its classic reproductions, Chippendale Chair Number 789, was selected for the collections of the Museum of American History at the Smithsonian Institution in Washington, D.C.

Bibliography

Armson, J., *The Encyclopaedia of Furniture*, London, 1938.
Aronson, Joseph, *The Encyclopedia of Furniture*, London, 1965.
————, *New Encyclopedia of Furniture*, New York, 1967.

Baker, Hollis S., *Furniture in the Ancient World*, London, 1966.
Battersby, Martin, *The World of Art Nouveau*, New York, 1968.
————, *The Decorative Twenties*, New York, 1969.
Bienenstock, Nathan I., *A History of American Furniture*, New York, 1970.
Boger, Louise A., *Complete Guide to Furniture Styles*, New York, 1969.
Bowman, John S., *American Furniture*, New York, 1985.
————, *Furniture Past and Present*, New York, 1966.
Boyce, Charles, *Dictionary of Furniture*, New York, 1985.
Bradford, Peter and Prete, Barbara (eds.), *Chair*, New York, 1978.
Butler, Joseph T., *American Antiques, 1800–1900: A Collector's History and Guide*, New York, 1965.

Cantor, Jay E., *Winterthur*, New York, 1985.
Clark, Robert Judson (ed.), *The Arts and Crafts Movement in America: 1876–1916*, Princeton, New Jersey, 1972.
Comstock, Helen, *American Furniture: A Complete Guide to Seventeenth, Eighteenth, and Early Nineteenth Century Styles*, New York, 1962.

Darling, Sharon, *Chicago Furniture: Art, Craft & Industry, 1833–1983*, New York, 1984.
Dormer, Peter, *The New Furniture*, London, 1987.

Eastlake, Charles L., *Hints on Household Taste in Furniture, Upholstery, and Other Details*, London, 1868.
Edwards, R., *The Shorter Dictionary of English Furniture*, London, 1964.
Edwards, R., and MacQuoid, P., *The Dictionary of English Furniture*, 3 vols., London, 1954.
Emery, Marc, *Furniture by Architects*, New York, 1983.

Flanagan, J. Michael, *American Furniture from the Kaufamn Collection*, Washington, D.C., 1986.

Gandy, Charles D., *Contemporary Classics: Furniture of the Masters*, New York, 1981.
Gandy, Charles D., and Zimermann-Stidman, Susan, *Contemporary Classics: Furniture of the Masters*, New York, 1981.
Garner, Philippe, *Contemporary Decorative Arts*, New York, 1980.
————, *Twentieth-Century Furniture*, New York, 1980.
Giedion, Sigfried, *Mechanization Takes Command*, New York, 1948.
Gloag, J. E., *English Furniture*, New York, 1965.
————, *A Social History of Furniture Design*, New York, 1966.

Hanks, David A., *Innovative Furniture in America from 1800 to the Present*, New York, 1981.

Harling, R. (ed.), *Modern Furniture and Decoration*, London, 1971.

Hayward, H. (ed.), *World Furniture*, London, 1965.

Hinckley, F. L., *A Directory of Antique Furniture*, New York, 1953.

Howe, Katherine S., and Warren, David B., *The Gothic Revival Style in America, 1830–1870*, Houston, Texas, 1976.

Ledoux-Lebard, D., *Les Ebénistes parisiens, 1795–1830*, Paris, 1951.

Liversidge, J., *Furniture in Roman Britain*, London, 1955.

Lucie-Smith, Edward, *Furniture: A Concise History*, London, 1985.

Lyon, Irving Whitall, *The Colonial Furniture of New England*, Boston, 1924.

McClinton, K., *An Outline of Period Furniture*, London, 1972.

Madigan, Mary Jean (ed.), *Nineteenth Century Furniture: Innovation, Revival and Reform*, New York, 1982.

Meadmore, C., *Modern Chairs*, London, 1973.

Mercer, E., *Furniture 700–1700*, London, 1969.

Miller, V. Isabelle, *Furniture by New York Cabinetmakers, 1650–1860*, New York, 1956.

Moody, E., *Modern Furniture*, London, 1966.

Naylor, Gillian, *The Bauhaus*, London, 1969.

Ormsbee, Thomas H., *A Field Guide to American Victorian Furniture*, Boston, 1964.

———, *A Field Guide to Early American Furniture*, Boston, 1951.

———, *The Story of American Furniture*, New York, 1934.

Osborne, Harold (ed.), *The Oxford Companion to the Decorative Arts*, New York, 1985.

Pevsner, Sir N. B. L., *Pioneers of Modern Design*, London, 1936.

Pile, John F., *Interior Design*, New York, 1988.

Praz, Mario, *An Illustrated History of Furnishing*, London, 1964.

Ransom, Frank Edward, *The City Built on Wood: A History of the Furniture Industry in Grand Rapids, Michigan. 1850–1950*, Ann Arbor, Michigan, 1955.

Richter G. M. A., *The Furniture of the Greeks, Etruscans and Romans*, London, 1966.

Russell, Frank; Garner, Philippe; and Read, John, *A Century of Chair Design*, New York, 1980.

Salazar, Tristan, *The Complete Book of Furniture Restoration*, New York, 1982.

Schaefer, H., *The Roots of Modern Design*, London, 1970.

Seale, William, *The Tasteful Interlude: American Interiors Through the Camera's Eye: 1860–1917*, New York, 1975.

Veronesi, Giulia, *Style and Design: 1909–1929*, New York, 1960.

Wanscher, O., *The Art of Furniture: 5,000 Years of Furniture and Interiors*, London, 1967.

Wilson, Richard Guy; Pilgrim, Dianne H.: and Murray, Richard N., *The American Renaissance, 1876–1917*, New York, 1979.

Wingler H. M. (ed.), *The Bauhaus*, Cambridge, Massachusetts, 1969.

Index

Photograph Credits

Harry N. Abrams, Inc. New York: 59

Antikenmuseum, Staatliche Museen, Preussischer Kulturbesitz, Berlin: 24 (top)

The Art Institute of Chicago: 34, 105

The Athens Museum: 21

Aves Advertising, Inc., Grand Rapids, Michigan: 33

Baker Furniture Company, Grand Rapids, Michigan: 31, 35–37, 39–41, 44, 45, 48, 49, 57, 60, 61, 69, 73, 75 (left), 86, 87, 126–129, 131–133, 136, 140, 141, 143–145, 148, 149, 152–160, 162, 163, 166

The Baltimore Museum of Art: 12, 84, 85

The Lee Boltin Picture Library: 19, 22

John Braden Watercolors: 138, 139

The Brooklyn Museum, Brooklyn, New York: 78

Caisse Nationale des Monuments Historiques et des Sites, Paris: 55

California Palace of the Legion of

Honor, San Francisco: 28, 56, 58 (lower right)

Christie's, New York: 112 (top)

Colonial Williamsburg Foundation: 9, 10, 71

Corvina Archives, Budapest: 98 (top)

Diderot Encyclopedia: 63

Editions du Regard, Paris: 112 (bottom), 113

The Egyptian Museum, Turin: 23

Furniture by Architects: 116, 118, 122

Galleria Nazionale d'Arte Moderna, Rome: 25 (top)

The J. Paul Getty Museum, Malibu, California: 62

Grand Rapids Art Museum, Grand Rapids, Michigan: 29, 92

The Greenfield Village and Henry Ford Museum, Dearborn, Michigan: 67

Hagmann Mitchell Architects: 93

Hancock Shaker Village, Pittsfield, Massachusetts: 14

Harter Corporation, Michigan: 123

The Hitchcock Chair Company,

Riverton, Connecticut: 90

Finn Juhl, Denmark: 119, 142

The Kaufman Collection: 65, 77

Knoll International, New York: 115, 117, 121, 125

Kunsthistorischen Museums, Vienna: 25 (bottom)

Kunstsammlungen der Veste Coburg: 32

Bernard & S. Dean Levy, Inc., New York: 70, 79, 82

Los Angeles County Museum of Art: 80

The Louvre, Paris: 26 (right), 52, 54

The Maryland Historical Society, Baltimore: 81, 94

The Metropolitan Museum of Art, New York: 27, 42, 43, 53, 58 (left), 66 (bottom), 74 (left), 83, 97, 99

Herman Miller, Inc. Archives: 120, 124

William Millington Watercolors: 134, 135

Museum of the City of New York: 11, 100, 101

Museum of Early Southern Decorative Arts, Winston-

Salem, North Carolina: 66 (top)

Museum of Fine Arts, Boston: 64, 74 (right), 75 (right)

The Museum of Modern Art, New York: 103

National Library of Medicine, Bethesda, Maryland: 51

The New York Historical Society: 102

The New York Public Library: 7

The Newark Museum: 96

The Philadelphia Museum of Art: 38 (bottom)

Sotheby Parke Bernet: 68

Staatliche Antikensammlungen, Munich: 24 (bottom)

Stair and Company, Inc., New York: 38 (top), 46, 47

The Tate Gallery, London: 95

Tiffany Studios: 107

The Mark Twain Memorial, Hartford, Connecticut: 98 (bottom)

Henry Francis du Pont Winterthur Museum: 15, 16, 17, 72

Zentralbibliothek, Zurich: 26 (left)